IN THE FOOTSTEPS OF JACK THE RIPPER

ALAN ROBSON MBE

BNBS

First published in 2017 by:
Britain's Next Bestseller
An imprint of Live It Publishing
27 Old Gloucester Road
London.
United Kingdom
WC1N 3AX

Cover design by Andrew Brewster

www.bnbsbooks.co.uk
@BNBSbooks

'To everyone who stayed loyal, my sincere thanks and blessings'

INTRODUCTION

Jack the Ripper was never caught.

... until now and you will follow two incredible strands of information, and solve it yourself! In the first book about the killer using the most modern forensic science, alongside the old world of spirit and mediumship.

We begin in the rather shabby Whitechapel area of London, back in late Victorian times inhabited by those without much. Grubby, paint peeling tenements, damp rotting homes that had all seen better days. The men, mostly unskilled doing basic manual work, their wives looking after the children at home. The other women choosing between market stalls, the horror of the workhouse or walking the streets as a prostitute. Many of the 'working girls' had been married but their men had left

them, and having lost the only form of income they had, they had to resort to perhaps the planets oldest profession.

There was a time when every male human being living in Whitechapel could have been declared a suspect in the grisliest set of murders that the capital had seen doing the time of Queen Victoria.

So how can we, after all this time, solve the crime that so many criminologists and authors have already taken a crack at? Well I decided to turn the hunt for 'Olde Jack' into a whodunit and let each one of you become the hunter, with one of the most devious killers of all time, as your gruesome prey.

Yet that is not enough, we need to do more. This means getting our feet on the ground, to literally be where 'he' was, experience all these years on, what 'he' experienced. We must walk in his footsteps.

I still felt that this was still not different enough from all the others who have gone before, intent on naming 'their' Jack the Ripper.

For the first time ever, modern forensic science mixed with spiritual investigation. I qualified as an exorcist in 2000, and have used the skills in many ways, yet never thought they would help in such an incredible journey. When hard research, modern day technology and the spirits unite, perhaps at last the real killer can be found?

CHAPTER ONE

Who was he?

How can any man rip women to pieces and yet remain invisible in the most crowded city in Europe?

Was it the infamous Masonic Plot?

Was it a conspiracy to protect a member of the Royal Family?

So many questions, so many misguided opinions and frankly a subject that is surrounded by so much spin and innuendo the truth has become inconsequential.

Do we prefer to wonder at the incredible disappearing act of one of humanities most sadistic butchers or, deep down, do we want to know the name of the man who was Jack the Ripper?

You will uncover the truth here and now.

CHAPTER TWO

Over the years we have watched countless movies all claiming to reveal the killer, yet if you follow the evidence they all actually fall well short.

So, let us begin with the obvious contenders.

The Duke of Clarence, known as Prince Eddy, was the second son of King Edward the Seventh and his name has become synonymous with the Ripper.

Why was that?'

Well, he was suspected of being bisexual and coach drivers speak of his penchant for 'enjoying the company of working boys' and girls'.

One doctor close to the Royals said that the Prince had contracted syphilis from his friends and this had transformed him into a criminal lunatic with violent tendencies.

His doctor Sir William Gull was said to have 'hushed up' many of his attacks on staff and public alike.

The other theory was that Prince Eddy married a common shop girl and she had a child.

The Prime Minister ordered fellow freemason Sir William Gull to mastermind the cover up. This involved the woman's murder, hidden amongst a serial killer's victims.

Gull was said to have drugged the girl to make her feeble minded and then placed her in a sanatorium for the rest of her days.

Yet the nanny, Mary Kelly one of the Rippers victims hatched a blackmail plot with her prostitute acquaintances. However, no child was ever uncovered so the story sounds like merely scuttle-butt and gossip.

The story of how Gull and a fellow doctor set out to silence them was later uncovered as a hoax.

Then the press started suggesting the Prince had impregnated Mary Kelly, yet according to her autopsy she was not with child.

Now, it is true that the Prince had a room in Watling Street where he and his fellow aristocrats could don disguises to walk amongst ordinary people (and frequent with

prostitutes). There was no proof of the orgies and violence the press had intimated.

All this and still no one looks at the basic evidence.

Was Prince Edward, the Duke of Clarence, without an alibi for his whereabouts on the nights that these women were killed?

The Prince has an alibi for each evening except one.

On one occasion, he was in Scotland 350 miles from the scene of the crime.

Could he be the Ripper, and using his power and position, gather those around him and make them prepared to lie for him?

In the 1990s a Sunday newspaper claimed they knew who the

Ripper was and proclaimed an exclusive. They named Dr Roslyn D'Onston as the killer.

None of the hugely well researched Ripper anthologies even mentioned this man, so is there any proof of his involvement?

Well, he was born Robert Donston Stephenson, the son of a mill owner in Hull.

He was a bit of a character; a drug addict, alcoholic, trouble-maker, Satanist and Doctor.

D'Onston did live in Whitechapel in 1888, so he would have a great knowledge of the tiny streets.

The murders were planned with great precision and this mysterious doctor had been a soldier earlier in his life.

As a doctor his knowledge of anatomy would certainly have been sufficient to find the specific organs targeted by the Ripper.

Whilst working as a journalist D'Onston claimed to know the Ripper and gave 'inside knowledge'. His knowledge of the occult said that the seven murder sites when plotted on a map fell in a fallen cross, an upside-down crucifix, declaring the killings a sacrifice to Satan. D'Onston said the Ripper was obviously trying to release a wave of negative psychic energy to give himself incredible dark powers.

The Doctor had studied the dark arts for twenty years, but was he merely lost in drug addled fantasies or was he really writing about himself?

The world famous black Magician Aleister Crowley claimed to have a box belonging to Jack the Ripper, full of bloodstained ties worn by the Ripper during each killing.

Yet the box originally belonged to Doctor Roslyn D'Onston.

This still does not prove him to be the Ripper, only that he had a fascination with the killings. Was it merely a ruse to give him status within the occult community?

Here is where the ONLY so called evidence of his involvement began.

A woman (unnamed), supposedly D'Onstons lover, claimed to have found the blood covered ties. She then admitted to the press that he had told her how he had administered chloroform to stop the women struggling and always ripped them from behind to avoid getting blood on him.

Yet, if this is so why soak his tie and leave evidence if he had tried so hard to avoid blood transference?

The police never interviewed this woman, and admitted that the journalist had told them she had been created to give credence to a theory.

The Doctor eventually succumbed to his advanced drug use, and illness claimed him.

He remained bed-bound, unable to walk or talk.

He was the perfect man to point the finger at as no one knows how or when he died.

Was he merely a fantasist trying to boost his position in the occult world by linking himself to the Ripper or was he responsible for those horrific murders?

CHAPTER THREE

As you see with only two suspects, three if you include the Prince's man Doctor William Gull, it is far from simple.

So, who else do we regularly mention when searching for a suspect?

Well in recent years the favourite was a man called Montague Druitt. He was a sexually insane barrister who loved sex with prostitutes.

His vigorous and violent sex acts with them included sodomy and choking, which brought him to the attention of the police.

Not long after the last Ripper murder he threw himself into the Thames and drowned.

Was this an admission of guilt or merely the inevitable result of insanity?

More questions fewer answers.

The police believed the killer had to be a doctor, nothing could sway them until the name of William Bury fell across their desk.

He was a murderer and was hanged for it.

Following his marriage, he had a punch up with his new wife in their digs and was stopped in the nick of time from cutting her throat with a razor.

During the Ripper's frenzy of killings, he walked into a police station to say his wife was dead. On visiting his house, they found writing on the wall claiming 'Jack The Ripper is behind this door'. There was another saying he was in the cellar.

There the police found his wife Ellen's body stuffed in a trunk, strangled and terribly mutilated. Her intestines were tugged through a gaping hole in her stomach.

Bury was hanged in Dundee in 1889. His vicious temper brought great attention to himself, surely he could not be the cool-headed Ripper?

So, what about George Chapman, who poisoned his three wives and owned a barbers shop in the middle of Whitechapel?

Following his arrest for killing his third wife, the police exhumed his first two and he was charged with their murders too. In Poland Chapman had worked, as a surgeon so knew his way around the human body.

Yet could a man who enjoyed the slow strangling of women really change his modus operandi to tearing them to pieces?

One of the surprise suspects was Aaron Cohen, who was arrested during a raid on a brothel. He showed extreme violence whilst in the cells and was placed in the Colney Hatch Asylum, where he attacked guards, nurses and tried to destroy his room.

Some say this man, also known as Nathan Kaminsky, driven mad through syphilis given to him by a prostitute. A good motive to want payback or merely a coincidence?

It is also thought that this man is often called Leather Apron as he worked as a skinner in a Slaughter yard.

There were many others, hundreds including Dr Thomas Cream a doctor and abortionist who we know poisoned four prostitutes.

There was Frederick Deeming who murdered his first wife and four children before becoming a prostitute addict.

Dr.Pedachenko, a Russian doctor was supposedly sent to London to murder women to embarrass the Government.

In recent years, American television show's became obsessed with finding anyone who had travelled there, who could have been the ripper. 'The American Ripper' found a man called H.H.Holmes, and a living relative claiming amazing details many unprovable, that he was the killer we all seek.

A life burglar George Neighbour was also considered as to being Jack. He broke into homes all over Whitechapel, but rarely from the well to do. If he was not the murderer, the police believed he would have a fair idea who it was.

In the 1950's a TV executive belonging to Fox claimed to have been contacted by the family of a journalist who had worked in the early 1900's in New England. Prior to a man's death, he asked the press to come to his deathbed and declared "I was Jack The Ripper!" The journalist, seeing dollar signs took it to print only for his family to say he was in Scotland when almost all the killings took place. His name was either Sullivan or O'Sullivan.

More questions, yet no one has looked at the basics.

Who was in Whitechapel at the time?

Who would lie to police seemingly for no reason?

Who knew the victims?

Who was seen by the public with the victims?

Who had a motive to kill them?

The only way to find out is to start from the very beginning and walk in the footsteps of Jack the Ripper!

CHAPTER FOUR

Perhaps the only way to get a true feel for the real horror that happened in Whitechapel is late at night through until the early hours of the morning.

The London police advised me that it is not the safest area to be in alone, late at night.

That is now, so how must it have been when there were so few street lamps, a myriad of small alleys, extreme poverty and so many murders that the police could frankly not cope?

Well, that is my first point 'so many murders', and this gives us our first direction.

In the 1960's Daniel Stein, of New York, worked as a college teacher, criminologist and expert in forensics, being used on numerous high profile cases as a profiler. He suggested our first course of action.

> "No murderer, as brutal and driven as Jack the

Ripper, just goes out there and kills with precision and planning" says Stein.

"You always find that they practice first, have episodes as a child or hint at the direction they are going. I have looked at the Ripper case and I see a man immersed in the people he is preying on. An anonymous face that people around think is pretty ordinary and safe.

A white male in his late twenties to early forties, who perhaps had a mother complex or was abused as a child. This person probably indulged in cruelty against animals and I can assure you that his first official attack was not his first crime. I am certain that he had killed before but in London at that time the authorities only ever pulled out all of the stops when someone from elite society was the victim. Life tor the poor was extremely tough and if these lower classes chose to kill each other, more often than not the murderer would get away with it. Even in bloody murder, money talks!"

Criminologist from Estonia Adama Fuchs wrote

> "I think it is very like what happened in recent years with the likes of Jimmy Savile. If you do things whilst totally under public scrutiny, it is stunning and almost in-comprehensive to believe you can get away with it-yet they do time and time again. If people know you, you therefore cannot be guilty, because they know you. Crimes like this had to be someone

else, an outsider creeping into this tight knit community before vanishing into the blood-soaked darkness. These people hide in broad daylight. In retrospect they should be easily caught!"

CHAPTER FIVE

So, my investigation brought me to the New Scotland Yard and Metropolitan Police Records of the time, wading through all of the murders in that area for five before the first 'official' Ripper murder, and there they are - the unsolved cases that bear definite signs of the practice' attack.

There is no way we can be sure exactly when this beast began. It is thought that he may have killed some of the animals that were abundant on the streets. Scruffy mutts and a myriad of flea ridden cats all living feral, literally scratching for a meal where they could. If they were to go missing, there would be no major outcry. During the three years up until we believe his real spree began it was common for cats to be found dead, impaled on railings, dogs with their throats slit, in some cases some of their insides removed. The police once gave a press briefing about how poor people were killing dogs, so they could eat their liver, kidneys etc "in an attempt to stay fed!"

What else happened around this same time?

Well a number of children went missing, all but a few never found. Some of these victims were described as 'street urchins'. Children without parents or family, living on the streets, usually thieving to feed themselves. If one was to disappear, the rest would see this as a price they paid to live that lifestyle. Billy Tatton from Whitechapel told a magistrate of that time "Well Mister sometimes you steals from the wrong feller, they track ye down and sorts you out. Some kills ya, and gets rid of your body. There are thems that you must be careful of if you lives like I do!". The magistrate asked for names, but the young lad held his tongue for his own security. However, three days after being released Tatton disappeared.

Was the Ripper building up, starting with animals, then the waifs off the street? It is more than likely. Anyone who became so gifted in bloody murder and mutilation surely needs to practise, to make his killings 'perfect'!

The first may have been a girl known as Betty. She was a bar worker in Whitechapel, having collected glasses in most of the cheaper low class establishments. One night she was out walking home from a late shift when a modus operandi we would later hear a lot of, may have had it's very first trial. As I walked this area now, there are still alleys and side streets I would rather not venture. Especially on foggy or misty nights. Yet back then these poor souls had to, it was where they lived, in the narrower and much dirtier accommodations of the time. On a long dark street, with streetlights almost 100 feet apart, the area between them was pitch black. In the middle, a man lay in wait, hiding in the doorway of a small tenement. As the girl scurried along a hand grasped her head, she felt something cold on her throat and screamed. Just then, two men walking around the corner heard her and raced towards the sound. Her attacker, a thick set chap, raced into the fog and gone. She checked her throat and it was nicked, but not cut. The men urged her to go to the police, but she refused. She would later tell of how some old drunk, smelling of ale had tried to 'do her'. Maybe she felt believing he waited sex was easier to carry than if he sought to kill her. Her employer also told her to go to the police; she refused and insisted that the barrel man walk her home each night.

The next was at very least attempted murder, it happened on Saturday the 25th of February 1888 when a rather plain factory worker Annie Millwood was found bleeding on the street and taken to hospital suffering from a dozen knife wounds to her torso. Her hands also bore defensive wounds for the savage attack she had defended so bravely.

She lived in White Row and was a war widow and known as a gentle soul.

She told police that a rather ordinary looking man had simply walked up to her, took an extremely sharp clasp knife from his pocket, knocked her to the ground and began stabbing her. Fortunately, it was a cold day and she had many thick layers of clothes on, and the knife had not been particularly sharp. Many of the stabs slid along the clothes rather than cutting through them.

In a shadowy corner of the street far from the dim streetlights and in London's fog there were no witnesses.

Week after week she seemed to be on the road to recovery, it had never crossed her mind that her attacker may seek to kill her. As she had taken a pretty good look at him, telling the police that he had looked 'sort of familiar'.

Months later she was released from the Workhouse infirmary, where she simply dropped dead. It is thought that the internal damage had weakened her and the official verdict from the coroner was 'The woman died from a sudden effusion into the pericardium from the rupture of the left pulmonary artery through ulceration'.

Essentially, it seems she died of blood poisoning caused by the blunt dirty knife.

The police filed this under 'death by natural causes' so it was lost in the files, never surfacing during the entire Ripper investigation, despite a detailed description given to police. The victim declared this man to be dressed in swarthy clothes, obviously not from any kind of wealthy background. She also added that her attacker was a man aged in his early thirties with an ordinary face and a moustache. About 5 foot seven inches and with bad skin. The biggest clue 'he seemed sort of familiar'!

A description that was a million miles away from the man they would spend their entire investigation searching for.

So, was this yet another Ripper rehearsal, where he perhaps lost his courage and failed to finish her off?

Would that frighten him off or merely make him more determined?

Well there were numerous other possibilities, like a seamstress who was attacked by a man in his thirties with a moustache and bad skin who demanded money and waved a knife at her, finally plunging it into her throat twice. A description given that yet again told of a tatty man, with poor clothes.

The woman, Ada Wilson, refused to hand over any cash then began screaming and swearing at her attacker. The police of the day refused to repeat the words she had used to the press, for it would be unseemly, and frankly a disgrace for any woman to choose. Yet her fighting back and those uproarious screams brought neighbours running from all directions. The man was lucky to escape. A dozen saw him make his escape. Spectators said, "He was running quick for a man of his size!"

The problem the police had was that there were hundreds of fights, attacks and knife fights all over the area at the time. They did not think it could just be one man at any time. Husbands stabbing wives, attacking men after a drink and a number of crime rings selling drugs, illicit drink or women. There seemed to be hundreds of reasons why people carried a weapon, even innocent folk may hold one for their own self-preservation

CHAPTER SIX

Was this a coincidence or merely the Ripper flexing his muscles and seeing just how far he could go?

If we judge him purely on the six established murders he appears to be a devilishly intelligent killer, yet looking back he could well have been rather clumsy and cack-handed in his earlier assaults.

Another woman, known only as Margaret, was grabbed from behind in Whitechapel in March 1888. She said she felt the man fumbling in his pocket, unable to get something out. At first she thought the man had rape on his mind, a remarkably common crime in London at that time.

This was a time when poor men could not afford even the price of a cheap working girl. However, she heard something metal fall on the wet cobbles as the man released his grasp to retrieve what she presumed to be a knife.

As he did she ran forward and on spotting several friends

screamed out that she was being attacked. When the men reached her the attacker had gone.

This was never reported to the police; only coming to light in the 1920s when the woman was on her deathbed.

It was a textbook Ripper attack move, from behind so he could not be splashed with blood.

How many others could he have practised on? This was a time when you did not grass, you tell the police nothing! So actual information on these crimes was very much word of mouth, and scarce even at that.

One attack each month seemed to be the Rippers technique and on a Bank Holiday Tuesday the 3rd of April 1888, Emma Smith, a 45-year old widow with two children, left her lodgings at 7.00pm to walk the streets.

She had no job yet managed to keep her family in food so was certainly a prostitute.

In the early hours one of her fellow working girls, Maggie Hayes, saw her walking to a man in his early thirties, about 5 foot eight wearing a dark, well-worn suit with a small scarf around his throat.

An hour or so later Emma was walking home when she was followed, robbed and raped by three men. Did the Ripper have allies?

On getting home it was obvious she needed to go to hospital. Her face badly bruised, her right ear had practically torn off, there were scratches on her face and she complained of a dull pain down below.

The poor woman had had a blunt object, perhaps a silver topped cane, or a 'thudder' a soft truncheon thrust inside her causing her perineum to rip needing eleven stitches.

Emma told police her story but later fell into a coma and died of her appalling injuries.

It is generally thought that it was a local gang, preying on prostitutes, who would not allow them to be their pimp.

Could the Ripper have been a member of a gang, or maybe the Ripper was not just one man. Once again, more questions than answers. Perhaps this one was not the Ripper at all.

No wonder the police, even at this time had no idea that this explosion of serial killing was about to explode upon Whitechapel's dark streets.

CHAPTER SEVEN

There were many more assaults, rapes and murders.

Most so badly investigated that there is no way of knowing whether the Ripper was involved or not. Some corpses at a local cemetery, that had been recently buried, had been mutilated around the lower body too. On one occasion 23 bodies were found mutilated and broken up, all recently buried. Two family tombs had been entered and human skulls taken. The police thought it was children or 'those following the dark arts. Yet was this Jack the Ripper, surely the darkest of all artists at that time?

Was this more practice or more smoke and mirrors?

Yet I am positive that the Ripper's first victim was a woman called Martha Tabram, who was found murdered by a dock worker at 4.40am on Tuesday the 7'" August 1888.

The sun was just about to rise and the workman saw the hapless soul lying on the hard, concrete stairs on a first-floor landing of George Yard.

She was on her back with her with her legs apart in an ever-growing pool of blood that trickled down the steps. Once on the pathway, the blood made its way around the edge of the harsh cobbles, and seemed to spread for yards in all directions.

When the police officer, Thomas Barrett, arrived at the scene, he presumed it was a sexual assault that had gone too far. He had seen many of those in his time.

Doctor Timothy Killeen was called to the scene to observe the body and pronounce her dead. In his report he declared that she had been brutally stabbed 39 times and may have had something inserted inside her intimate areas. The post mortem would reveal all.

In the police constables report he also said that he had questioned a man at around 2am, who was late twenties/early thirties with a moustache and bad skin. He had found the man standing in a darkened doorway and told the policeman that his friend had 'gone off with a whore' and he was waiting for him. This was a common enough practice in that part of town so the Constable had walked on. The woman was murdered around 2.45am.

It seems a number of others had walked passed Martha's body having seen it.

When it was dark in Whitechapel it was quite common to see the slumped bodies of drunks. In some cases, equally drunken men would rape these poor inebriated ladies. Any trying that with poor Martha would have had a shock.

In the Coroners Court Dr. Killeen told the throng that there were 22 stab wounds to Martha's torso, her left lung had been burst with five wounds, causing it to crash, and the right lung was sliced into two pieces.

The liver had five deep insertions, the stomach had been penetrated six times, the spleen twice and there had been one forceful stab wound in her heart.

There was one deep wound in the vagina and yet the doctor did not mention the wounds to her throat and thighs, nor that facial scratching. It seems he was struggling to control her because of her size, and ended up clawing at her eyes.

The surprising thing was that it was claimed that the woman did not struggle, making the Doctor believe that she was perhaps rendered unconscious before the savage killer went to work on her. Yet had she not struggled why was she so scratched and bruised?

The following day the press declared the killer had medical knowledge, yet the Doctor had made no mention of this and did not think he did have medical knowledge of any kind. A fellow surgeon said that the wounds seemed to be scattered in the general direction of various organs as if attempting to hit them all. This had very much been anatomy for beginners?

A local army barracks was investigated without anything conclusive.

The body had been identified by her ex-husband, who had left her because of her drinking. Enter Inspector Frederick Abberline - the main detective who would pursue Jack the Ripper would later admit that he also believed Martha to be his first official victim.

Especially when Chief inspector Swanson later admitted Martha had nine separate stab wounds to her throat, given by a man standing behind her and throttling her whilst holding her down.

The pattern of what was to come had been perfected?

Three weeks later, perhaps inspired by his earlier success with Martha Tabram, Jack the Ripper started his official tour.

CHAPTER EIGHT

It was just after 3.30am when Charlie Cross (also called Charles Allen Lechmere) a cart driver was walking to work and spotted a dirty tarpaulin in the gateway of Brown's Stable Yard in Bucks Row.

He knew that it would block the carts, so was about to tug it out of the way when he discovered it was actually a woman, lying in a heap on the wet ground.

His fellow worker, Robert Paul, saw him looking down and went to investigate.

The obvious presumption was that it was another drunk who had not made it home.

On taking a closer look they saw that her skirts were raised, so then they agreed she had probably been raped.

The poor working girls of that time had no choice but to accept that rape was a hazard of their profession in that part of Victorian London. Yet most punters would never kill the girl, even if they would rape them. They all knew that even raped they did not trust the police, nor would they grass.

On touching her hand he knew she was dead so they pulled the woman's skirt down and walked off to find a policeman.

By the time they had found one another Constable had already uncovered the body of Mary Ann Nichols. As he shone a torch into her pale face he could see that blood was still slowly oozing from her slit throat.

Dr. Llewellyn determined that the woman had only been dead for about thirty minutes, meaning that when she was first found she was actually still alive and perhaps could have been saved. By presuming her dead, Charlie Cross had actually killed her!

The mortuary was opened especially for the body to be taken in.

On lifting her skirt the doctor discovered that the lower body had been terribly mutilated. The stomach had been torn open to reveal the intestines.

The attendant vomited on seeing it as Dr. Llewellyn admitted it was the most brutal case he had ever seen. It took over forty minutes before his staff could remove the body, as they were so shocked at having to collect the intestines, and each man was soaked in blood. How would it be possible for her murderer not to be?

Her poor clothing speaks volumes for the social position of poor Mary Ann Nichols.

She was wearing a tatty coat with brass buttons, a brown woollen frock, a cotton undergarment, two petticoats, a pair of stays, black wool stockings and a pair of men's boots that were obviously second hand. One had the price written on the tatty scuffed sole.

She had a battered old straw bonnet and she had stolen one of her petticoats from Lambeth Workhouse, as it still bore its name.

All she had in her purse was a comb, a white handkerchief and the broken corner from a mirror. In the corner of a ripped pocket, there was a card with three colours of thread wrapped around and a big needle.

At the post mortem, Dr. Llewellyn's report was to the point and dramatically to the point.

> 'The body was that of a female 40 to 45 years of age. Her face was horribly bruised with one dark mark running along the lower part of the jaw on the right-hand side. A fist or the pressure of a thumb may have caused this mark. Her tongue was lacerated as she was throttled, leaving it almost in two. Another bruise on the left side seemed to be caused by fingers. On the left side of the neck below the jaw was an incision 4 inches long running from directly below the ear. A second cut, but deeper an inch below that one that went right across to the other ear. This had completely severed all of the tissues down to the vertebrae and the carotid arteries on both sides of the neck were severed. It was a strong bladed knife, moderately sharp and used with great violence.
>
> On the lower part of the abdomen, there was a very deep wound that ran in a jagged manner cutting through the tissue. There were four other cuts running downwards on the right side, the knife having been used violently. The killer has some rough anatomical knowledge for they attacked all the

> vital parts. Yet this entire crime could easily have been committed in less than five minutes.'

If this were true, surely the killer would be crimson in blood from head to toe! Face it experienced surgeons of the day still find themselves splashed by a patient's blood.

Later the good doctor said he believed that the killer may have been trying to obtain some of the woman's organs, but had been disturbed. This is backed up by the fact that when she was discovered she was still alive, blood still flowing from her wound. Sadly, she could not survive the mutilations done to her by a man who knew exactly what he wanted to achieve. Terror!

Terror on the streets, headlines in the press and all about this deranged outsider! Whitechapel prided itself on its community spirit, rough and ready folk who looked after one another.

It is almost certain that the Ripper saw the man walk into Bucks Row and escaped into the shadow before finishing his loathsome handiwork.

Once again, the press had a field day. Another killer who was 'obviously' a doctor.

The press can translate 'a rough knowledge' into a professional surgeon.

The police were being guided in the wrong direction. Yet they never seemed to question it. Later they would ask why, yet was someone powerful involved and organising some form of cover up? A million suggestions, all from people seeming not to have a clue.

Once again a busy and crowded part of London and yet no one heard a sound.

For years, those who lived in the wrong part of town had

learned to ignore what goes on in the shadows. Gangs battling for control, robberies, rapes, sex with prostitutes.

All things that decent people tried to distance themselves from.

In yet another case, the police had no help, only hindrance from the press, directing them to some rich doctor. The poor residents were of course happy to blame the class divide and campaign against the police for not caring for the poor.

At this time, there was no furore, no clamouring from the public to find the killer.

In fact, the death of prostitutes was so common place the local paper put the story on page five, but had said that the killer 'ripped into her'.

Many believe that this was the beginning of a nickname that would live on forever.

It would be the Ripper's next victim that would begin a frenzy of activity. when the press

realised that it was Britain's first true serial killer.

A character they would make an international celebrity.

CHAPTER NINE

GHOST HUNT NUMBER ONE

BUCK'S ROW where poor Mary Anne Nichols body had lain no longer exists. It is now a modern thoroughfare known as Durward Street, Whitechapel. In early October 1998 I gained access to the brick building overlooking where the yard had been and placed a camera and recording apparatus there. The camera showed orbs and a few odd light anomalies. The recording actually got a noise that could have been a horse, at a time when it was certainly a cars only area. Throughout the night, there was a recurrence of a bizarre white light that kept shining into the room, staying a while before disappearing. A few car headlights yet this light was different. Other than that, what we obtained was benign. Yet that light was strange.

GHOST HUNT NUMBER TWO July 2017

IN EARLY JULY 2017 I returned and gained access to that brick building, directly looking down at the area where the gate to Buck's Row had been. This time the room, redecorated and modern had a definite edge. There felt to be a distinct heaviness to the atmosphere. Often you get this at a place where great harm or murder has been done, yet it was noticeably absent on my first visit. I positioned a recording device and got heavy footprints, what sounded like heavy breathing. If that had been Jack, could this mean that the Ripper had been watching Mary Ann Nichols for a few days, knowing that she often took punters into Bucks Row to 'service' them? From this building, he could have watched her for days. It seems to be perhaps our first spiritual lead. Face it, it was at least as possible as some of the theories given by the press!

SIGHTINGS:

OVER THE YEARS those working in Durward Street have witnessed hundreds of cases of 'black entities' moving along the street at night. In homes and businesses there have been a lot of ghostly sightings. One of the most commonly reported was the sound of an old Victorian dress 'shishing' along corridors. Moving through rooms whilst the occupants were in bed, but listening carefully to this very distinct noise. Some locals captured it on tape, yet it was never linked to the Ripper killing on that very street. At a local shop on the street a sales worker Jean Barton said "I've had trouble since working here, it is obviously haunted. When the shop is closed things fire off shelves, we have seen this on our CCTV. The boss thought I was doing it to wind him up because he is frightened of such things, yet I thought he was doing it to me!"

In 2016 Richard & Anne Sullivan from Belfast were staying on the street with friends for a few nights when Anne heard a woman screaming outside the window. She raced across to the window, dialling 999 on her mobile phone. She could see two people, barely black shapes fighting on exactly where Bucks Row used to have been. She told the police "The man looks quite chunky he's wearing what looks like a dark suit of some kind, maybe tweed. He has a hat on, like a top hat but not so tall. The woman has a long hippy skirt on, and he is really battering her. After that first scream she is saying nothing just taking it". Just then the man looked both ways and started walking in long strides along to the edge of the street and along a side street.

The police arrived and there was no injured woman, who, according to both Sullivan's "evaporated whilst we waited for the police".

Was this history replaying exactly what the Ripper did? They both saw it, so it was not imagination. The most interesting thing was that the Sullivan's nor their friends the Robinson's knew that a Ripper killing had taken place in that street. That was the very reason the Council renamed it Durward Street.

There are hundreds of sightings on this street every year. The number is probably exacerbated by the sheer number of Ripper followers seeking out a visit to all of his murder sites. Discount ninety five percent, you only need 1% for it to be true. There is a chill feel here even on a hot day, and after dark becomes a very intimidating place.

CHAPTER TEN

We return to our Ripper murder timeline!

Nine days after his last murder he was ready to kill again.

At 5.00am John Richardson entered the back yard at 27 Hanbury Street, using a hand knife to cut a loose bit of leather of a boot that he had hand cobbled. Local carpenter Albert Cadosch had entered the yard next door 29 Hanbury Street around 5.30am. When interviewed by the police he told them "I heard voices from the yard next door, a man and a woman. I had heard many over the years, doxy's (prostitutes) with their mark, looking for somewhere quiet. Normally they were long gone by the time all us market lads started to make a move. Just as I readied to leave I heard something heavy fall up against the fence. But thought it could have been the couple finishing their business!"

John Davis was a porter at Spitalfields Market and this meant he had to be at work by 6.30am. On leaving his digs at 5.45am as he walked down that yard eating some bread, when he saw someone lying between the steps and the fence. He bent down to see if it was someone drunk or passed out, only to discover the blood-soaked corpse of Annie Chapman. At first he stared at this awful picture, he had never seen death up close before. At first, he just wanted to step over her body, let someone else find it, but finally he dragged his wits together, and shouted loudly for the police. Soon people came running and a police officer's whistle was blown.

Inspector Joseph Chandler rushed to the scene; his graphic report demonstrated how the killer's barbarity was increasing with his celebrity.

Chandler wrote

> 'I proceeded to 29 Hanbury Street and in the back yard found a woman lying on her back, dead, left arm resting on her breast, legs drawn up, abducted, small intestines and flap of the abdomen lying on the right side, above the right shoulder attached by a cord to the rest of the intestines inside the body. Two flaps of skin from the lower part of the abdomen were lying in a large quantity of blood above the left shoulder. The throat had been cut deeply from the left and back in a jagged manner around the throat.'

A Doctor Phillips would add to his report

> 'The face was swollen as if beaten and the tongue protruded through the front teeth'

Next to the body was a torn fragment from her shawl, a small tooth comb, a pocket comb, an envelope with a stamp from 'The

Sussex Regiment' and above them on the wall a huge smear of blood as if the killer had sought to wipe his hand.

Three days later a man known as Leather Apron, John Pizer, was arrested and they recovered five long knives at his property.

As he worked with knives in his profession, this was not really a surprise, but it may have kept the heat off the police while they continued their investigations.

During the inquest, Annie's last movements were described.

When Annie had returned at 1.45am, she settled down in front of a low fire to eat a baked potato. She had been asked for her doss money but could not pay; she had explained that she could not find a John that night. She had tried to borrow off other girls without success. Yet she had told her friend, a local night watchman that she had been to see her sister in Vauxhall.

Leather Apron was eventually released without charge and the police arrested Jacob Isenschmid, as some Londoners were claiming that no Englishman could be responsible for such a horrific murder.

The press demanded that 'the murderous foreigner must be found' and then declared that the mutilations were obviously done by a doctor.

Many of the police of the day were simple men, short on training.

Many of these men viewed the police force as a way to get out of the squalor of their relatively poor lives. I think many of them were affected by blanket newspaper coverage that always seemed to steer them the wrong way. Especially as they lived amongst the people who were constantly complaining about the Europeans who lived amongst them or the sizeable Jewish population who always appeared well off whilst they were in rags.

The press had a field day when the autopsy details were

published as the Ripper's mode of murder was fully exposed. Hundreds of leads and postcards were sent to the police and local press supposedly being from the killer. Including one in very specific handwriting, proclaiming it to be from 'Saucy Jack'

He had found a shadowy spot in that dark yard, punched her to the ground leaving bruises to her temple and began to strangle her until she was semi-conscious.

Then before she could struggle, slit her throat from behind.

This would keep the blood spurt from hitting him.

Some of Annie's rings were missing yet this could have been from a previous day, as often working girls had to pawn belongings to pay rent. It could also have been anyone passing, as locals desperately short of money and living in extreme poverty had robbed many dead and drunken bodies in the street.

CHAPTER ELEVEN

On the 27th September 1888 another letter in similar handwriting arrived at Scotland Yard:

'DEAR BOSS

I keep on hearing the police have caught me but they wont fix me just yet. I have laughed when they look so clever and talk about being on the right track. That joke about Leather Apron gave me real fits. I am down on whores and I shan't quit ripping them till! get buckled. Grand work the last job was. I gave the lady no time to squeal How can they catch me now. I love my work and want to start again. You will soon hear of my funny little games. I saved some of the proper red stuff in a ginger beer bottle over the last job to write with but it went stiff like glue and I cant use it Red ink is fit enough I hope ha ha. The next job I shall clip the ladies ears off and send to the police officers just for jolly wouldn't you. Keep this letter back till! do more work, then give it out straight. My knife's so nice and sharp I want to get to work right away if I get a chance.

Good Luck Yours Truly Jack the Ripper

Don't mind me giving the trade name.

PS Wasn't good enough to post this before I got all the red ink oil my hands curse it They say I'm a doctor now ha ha.'

WHOEVER WROTE this had little or no medical knowledge as it came as a surprise that blood would clot. So, if the Ripper did write these letters he was obviously uneducated and not a doctor, yet still almost all their enquiries were in that area.

Could they have been a double bluff, a doctor trying to appear uneducated and a novice in all things anatomical?

CHAPTER TWELVE

At that time, the press were not told that an attempt had been made to cut off Annie's head. This suggests that the Ripper certainly was not a butcher or tanner who had a simple technique for doing this. Any doctor would also have known how.

The newspapers only heard that the uterus, vagina and two thirds of the bladder had been removed.

This led to headlines like 'Doctor Death back on the streets of Whitechapel' and 'The Ripper Returns'.

The police, to their credit, were trawling to catch this psychopath, visiting the Sussex Regiment to find out who knew Annie.

Soldier's handwriting was examined, none matched the envelope.

Then it was discovered that locals bought those envelopes because the nearest post office was miles away. So literally anyone, an insider or outsider, could have purchased any number. Especially if they wanted to blame one of the multitude of military people living and serving in the City.

To add to the misconception, Dr. Phillips was asked outright if the killer was a member of his profession. His answer was 'Well the murderer does seem to have anatomical knowledge' yet later in his conversation added that he thought it 'most unlikely'.

However, the press used the quote that fitted their story and ignored the good doctor's addition.

CHAPTER THIRTEEN

A postcard arrived at the News Agency on the 1st October 1888 in the same hand as the previous letters.

'I WAS NOT CODDLING dear old boss when I gave you the tip, you'll hear about Saucy Jacky's work tomorrow, double event this time number one squealed a bit couldn't finish straight off. Had not got time to get ears for police thanks for keeping the letter back till I got back to work again.

Jack the Ripper.'

WITHIN 24 HOURS the bodies of Liz Stride and Catherine Eddowes were recovered.

Five days later on the 6th October Jack became angry and once again in the same hand sent a threatening letter.

'YOU THOUGHT *yourself very clever I reckon when you informed the police. But you made a mistake if you thought I dident see you. Now I know you know me and I see your little game, and I mean to finish you and send your ears to your wife if you show this to the police or help them if you do I will finish you. It no use your trying to get out of my way. Because I have you when you don't expect it and I keep my word as you soon see and rip you up.*

Yours truly Jack the Ripper.'

PS You see I know your address.'

IT WAS SENT to one of the witnesses who retracted his statement but did hand the letter to the police. The killer, Jack the Ripper, obviously lived in Whitechapel and knew who was saying what and where they lived.

A letter from Galashiels in Scotland, that would lead to the police suspecting Scot James Maybrick, a Liverpool Merchant of being the killer read:

'DEAR BOSS

I have to thank you and my Brother in Trade, Jack the Ripper for your kindness in letting me away out of Whitechapel. I am now on the road to the tweed factories. I will let the Innerliethen Constable or police men know when I am about to start my little game. I have got my knife replenished so it will answer both Ladies and Gents. Other 5 tweed ones and I have won my wager.

I am yours

Truly

Jack the Ripper.'

WAS THIS A COPYCAT, as no Scottish murders would match the Ripper's fingerprints?

Was it merely a holiday where the killer toyed with the police dragging them away from London?

CHAPTER FOURTEEN

GHOST HUNT ONE:

IN THE LATE nineties Hanbury Street was a bustling street, with many empty buildings, and a good seventy shop fronts. So I positioned a sound recorder in the yard, directly in the corner where poor Annie was despatched. It was left on record from around 2.00am until 7.00am a good twenty minutes after the deed had been done. I captured footsteps, a gang of men giggling and shoving each other about, and more interestingly the clear sound of a woman saying "I know you!".

Now this had no footsteps leading up to it, it was a woman's voice, in the middle of an empty backstreet. Surely had this been any random woman you would hear her coming, and you would hear her leave. If it had been someone from the flats upstairs from the shops, you would hear a window or a door open and close. Was this another clue from beyond the grave, suggesting Annie Chapman knew her killer!

GHOST HUNT 2: JULY 2017

HANBURY STREET SEEMS to have changed a little since last I walked it. The little hollow where I placed my audio recorder was still there. I put it in the same place at roughly the same time, retrieving it around 9.30am the following morning. Once again you hear a few of the late night crew mooching about. I even caught what sounded like an aggressive drug deal going down. The last time I had caught a voice that I would love to believe was that of Annie Chapman herself. So I was not confident of beating that. Yet at precisely 5.34am there is a disembodied scream on the tape. Once again no footsteps or doors opening, just coming from the air. The scream sounded stifled after a couple of seconds. Was I being guided from beyond the grave towards the true murderer. It would certainly not surprise me that these poor ladies in spirit would not be able to rest until their killer had been outed. Was it some local who saw me planting the tape who just wanted to spin me a fishy story. Either way on hearing that scream, sounding similar in voice to the woman I had caught saying "I know you!". Like criminology, working with spirit is filled with frustration.

SIGHTINGS:

THERE HAVE BEEN many ghostly sightings in this area too. The most regular entity is that of a woman wearing a long black dress, with a small black bonnet 'floats' along a path. Hundreds can testify to seeing her. She began in about 1910 and people continued seeing her as recently as June 2017. Is this Annie Chapman in a carefree jaunt heading directly to her slaughter?

In the buildings nearby, one office had an exorcism because 'something' was trashing the place after everyone else had gone home. The place was given a priests blessing, but the activity increased, so the manager brought in an exorcist. The premises were finally cleared and remain free of external otherworldly interference.

The News of the World newspaper once ran a story from a local on Hanbury Street, complaining that late at night he regularly heard women screaming. Yet even when he angrily raced into the street to shut them up, they were long gone. Another local informed the newspaper that it was the site of a Ripper slaying and the story travelled across the globe!

CHAPTER FIFTEEN

The hunt continues, and we get closer every step!

Most Ripper writers over the years only ever dealt with the five Ripper murders, as shown in the records from Victorian times. Yet why didn't they look into the other records of the day, to see what may have been missed or hidden?

For just over week after Annie's murder there were two other attacks on Commercial Road, Whitechapel.

A prostitute called Susan Ward had worked hard that night, dozens of clients, and with her hard-earned cash had decided to get herself completely drunk.

Dozens of witnesses watched her staggering around, singing and making a fool of herself. When men approached her wanting sex, she threw up her dress and waved her underwear at them screaming "That's all you'll get tonight sweetness… tonight I'm taking for myself!" Yet later that night she was in the alley of the pub, almost comatose with the amount she had drank. She was so drunk some men were having their way with her in turns whilst she just giggled and said 'Help Yourself'.

As any hardened drinker will tell you, there are things that will sober you up in a hurry.

As she walked home, in anything but a straight line, a man lurched out of the shadows grasping her throat. When she saw a knife in his hand suddenly, her strength and wits returned.

He tried to slice open her throat but she put her arm up and the knife cut into that.

His grip on her wavered as she writhed herself free and screamed.

It was a busy night and the footsteps of people running towards the sound forced the attacker to run off.

Trying to keep down the panic sweeping the streets the police told the press this was unrelated to the Ripper. Yet it fits the pattern of weekend attacks, the technique was precise and there was a living witness. Because of her drunkenness and her totally belligerent attitude towards the police no formal statement was ever taken.

Spin from the police was making it hard to solve the crime, particularly when added to the downright lies told by the press and the gossip on the streets.

Information was coming forward from all sides. Yet what did Susan Ward actually remember through the drunken haze?

Her best friend Elizabeth Sneddon did talk to the police, for she was told by Susan that her attacker was wearing a tatty dark suit. The face was familiar, as if she had seen him around but it was purple with fury that made him harder to recognise.

Apparently, the prostitute may even have asked her pimp and members of their gang to find him and sort him out. I am certain this was another unsuccessful attack whilst the history books choose to make the Ripper seem infallible.

Had this attack been thoroughly investigated, I believe it could have been his last one.

Also that night, according to a local barman at a local tavern, around ten minutes after the attack on Susan Ward, a female itinerant, was knocked over by a man in a dirty suit, waving a long knife at her. When she looked at his startled face, he drew a scarf across his lower face, and darted past her into the fog.This happened at the opposite end of Commercial Road, Whitechapel.

Was this the Ripper, finally outed, having remained hidden whilst the police attended Susan Ward? Had he been forced to stay where he was until the furore died down? Then as she was taken off to hospital, he rushed away the opposite way, bundling into this homeless woman. She was in her late fifties and she was so concerned she told a beat police officer what happened. He merely told her to move along. Is it any wonder Jack was roaming free?

CHAPTER SIXTEEN

Apart from the witnesses that I have listed there were of course "The Ripper Letters'. Between the attacks on Susan Ward and Liz Stride a letter was sent to the Central News Agency. It read:-

'DEAR BOSS

So now they say I'm a Yid when will thay !ern Dear old Boss. You and me know the truth don't we. Lusk can look forever hell never find me but I am rite under his nose all the time. I watch them looking for me and it gives me fits ha ha. I love my work and I shant stop until I get buckled and even then watch out for your old pal Jacky. Catch me if you can.

Jack the Ripper.

PS Sorry about the blo'od still messy from the last one. What a pretty necklace I gave her.'

AS SUSAN WARD survived he was referring to Annie Chapman's cut throat, or perhaps that he had thrown her attached entrails over her shoulder. The police and press thought that this was unlikely to be the killer. After all he could not even use basic punctuation, his spelling was appalling and this did not fit the profile of a rich gentleman.

CHAPTER SEVENTEEN

Two weeks later, on Sunday 30th September 1888 , just around the corner from Commercial Road, in a van and cart builders yard called Outfields, Louis Diemschutz was going in to work. He was the steward of the Workers Club in the adjacent Dutfields Yard.

He turned his pony and cart into the yard as the animal began to shy as there was a dark shape lying on the ground.

He carried on; telling his boss there was someone sleeping it off in the yard.

Sadly, that was not the case. Instead they had stumbled across the mutilated and broken body of Elizabeth Stride.

The police and Doctor were there in minutes and the body was still warm, it had not been long since she had been despatched.

This is the best time for obtaining evidence.

As it was just after 1am oil lamps were brought to illuminate the gory scene, creating a glowing mist that seemed to drift along the blood-soaked lane.

Her right hand was over her chest yet covered in her blood, the left hand was on the ground and held a packet of cachous (a lozenge for sweetening the breath, used by prostitutes of the time to obscure the bad breath of some of their clients) wrapped in tissue paper.

As the doctor examined her, some spilled out bouncing across the stone floor, and trickling into the cracks between the slabs.

The woman's face looked very calm, yet the scarf she wore had been pulled very tightly around her neck as if her attacker had used that to throttle her before committing the murder.

The bottom of the scarf had been frayed for the killer had used the bottom edge as a guide as he drew the knife across her throat.

The Doctor, Frederick Blackwell, concluded that she had been dead less than thirty minutes. This meant almost certainly that the Ripper was nearby.

The victim was a tall, slightly classier prostitute Elizabeth Stride, a woman who had her own coffee shop, until her marriage broke down. Once that happened her man sold everything, took it and left her on the streets to manage as best she could.

She ended up in the workhouse and regularly suffered bronchitis from the dust, so to make up her wages she began working on the streets. A decision that would cost her life.

Yet this was not the only murder of this same night. Because he had been unable to mutilate his victim, his insatiable lust for blood had certainly not been fully satisfied.

Yet a crowd was gathering, staring at the poor body, her clothes soaking in the light drizzle that fell, her blood mixing with rain and running down a grid full of leaves and rubbish. They tried, without disturbing the body, to place her on a cart, covering her with an old blanket.

It seems that to the Ripper killing a girl without mutilating her, was like sex without an orgasm. The night still had time and there were many other women walking around 'on offer' at that time of night. If fact because the Ripper had already murdered it made other prostitutes more confident about going out to solicit sex. After all he's already killed!

No one expected what happened next!

CHAPTER EIGHTEEN

GHOST HUNT 1

THE SITE of Liz Stride's murder today is a long road, regularly patrolled by traffic wardens. Five storey blocks of flat's with insufficient parking, must make this road a double yellow lined gold mine for the authorities. On the side of the road where Liz was killed there are high walls and locked iron gates. Yet using an old map from the time established where her poor body had lain. I placed a recording device. On this we captured many cars, vans, trucks, road sweepers, passers-by and one piece of heavy-breathing when there seemed to be so one about.

GHOST HUNT 2 JULY 2017

ON RETURNING TO THE SCENE, I was rather surprised at how much busier that it had become. Even in the early hours of the morning, partygoers, and drinkers, lots of cars, buses, trucks, and refuse collectors with the noise of beeps as it reversed to collect wheelie bins. They were very loud and yet there is a whispered sentence over traffic, yet without anyone walking nearby. At first I thought, on slowing the tape, it said 'MONICA IN TROUBLE' yet on getting back to a professional studio, it say's 'GOT HE'S MONICA ON COBBLE'. This made no sense to me at all. Yet on talking about it to a local police detective on the Northumbrian force, he said "You do know that in past times a person's moniker was a slang word for someone's name!"

Firstly, this whisper may be nothing to do with the entire Ripper investigation. Yet if the spirits are active and want me to solve this case, could it have been that Liz, had written a slang name for her killer on a cobble, or his initials?

Had it been in blood it would have washed off in the rain? Had she carved it on a cobble it was never found at the time? I asked the Council what happened to the cobbles that used to be there, to be told, "We'd bring them back to the yard, then use them to replace other cobbles in other places when necessary. Those went, I think to Buckingham Palace!"

So could a cobble in Buckingham Palace have the Ripper's name on it? We may never know. Yet if she did write a slang name for this man, she obviously had known him very, very well! If this is true, it narrows the search down massively!

SIGHTINGS:

THIS IS a busy thoroughfare and yet there are a few regular sightings in the street. One being a young child dressed in a raggy shirt, a cardigan and shorts. Some say it is the spirit of a little boy Ian Evans who died in the blitz in 1941.

It is said that much of the area had been flattened by German bombs; a number of fires still were burning when the local children ran out of the shelters to collect shrapnel. Ian spotted a huge lump in the bottom of a crater, so jumped down. A local A.R.P. warden shouted at him to get out of there. The 'shrapnel' was part of the covering to an unexploded bomb, when the child grabbed it half the road exploded, firing skin and flesh spurting blood all over the warden. Young Evans still plays around there, usually on twilight nights, when the air is moist and foggy.

There is a female 'silkie' a woman in a long dress that is often seen on the street, she looks rather tatty and unkempt, and swans along the street with real attitude. She has been photographed by the press and public alike, and witnessed by many, just before turning translucent and disappearing.

Is this Liz Stride, who was known for confidence and being rather over the top?

Take in the details, as we head on crashing towards our face to face with the real Ripper!

CHAPTER NINETEEN

So back to that foggy night and it seems obvious that the Ripper had been disturbed, probably by the pony and cart plodding towards the yard. This gave the killer sufficient time to escape into the shadows before he could entertain himself by mutilating his victim. That was so obviously his favourite part, and he would not be satisfied until that deed was done. More death was on its way.

By this time, Inspector Abberline had been given full control of the case, and this night he was already racing around Whitechapel like the lunatic he was chasing. He was a trusted police officer with a good mind, rather prone to solid police plodding rather than speed, not helped by the facts of the case being distorted by everyone.

The police were spinning the story to reduce its impact on the public, the press wrote whatever lie would generate sales, the public continued to believe it was a foreigner. Probably a Jewish butcher or doctor. They were soft targets; there were enough racists locally who would be happy to blame any Jew or foreigner for this and any other crime going!. They were so proud of their cockney clique that they refused to believe any insider could do this type of thing to their own.

To show you how easy it was to waste police time based on innuendo, they searched for five days for a man called Lipski as people kept saying 'Lipski is responsible'.

So they had to investigate, but could not find anyone of that name.

Inspector Abberline was the man who stopped the inquiry. He knew that Lipski was not the name of a person; it was what the locals of Whitechapel called any Jew. Racists who felt that the Jewish community had all the money and were jealous of their success used this derogatory term. So one uneducated person heard someone yell 'Lipski is the Ripper' and presumed Lipski was a person. Hundreds would write to the police or tell officers this, without ever realising, they were being racist against all Jews. All it takes is one prejudiced individual to start something, and the ignorant hordes will follow suit!

LET us look at the facts and the real evidence in the case of Elizabeth Stride.

A man called James Brown saw Liz and a potential punter at the bottom of the road.

The man was unkempt, quite fat and wore a long coat down to the ground, with a high scarf around his face.

Liz was heard to say "No not tonight... how ever we could do some other night" and the man walked away.

About thirty minutes later Constable William Smith saw Liz, recognisable by a flower she wore on her jacket. He saw Liz with a man in a deerstalker hat and dark, rather tatty looking clothes. He was late twenties or thirties and clean shaven carrying a newspaper parcel in his hand. It was about 18 inches long and 6 to 8 inches wide.

If this was the Ripper he was not wealthy, for no one other than a common man would carry such a crude parcel. Newspaper was the wrapping of a man not prepared to pay for it to be done properly.

At the murder scene an in depth, listing was made of what was around the body.

Elizabeth Stride was about 42 years old, five feet two inches with curly dark brown hair.

Her eyes were light grey and her front two teeth were missing. She was wearing a long black jacket trimmed with dark fur, an old black skirt and a dark brown velvet bodice. Add to those two rather old petticoats, a white chemise and white stockings.

This look was topped with a black bonnet, boots and pinned to her lapel a single red rose.

All she had on her in the form of actual possessions were two handkerchiefs, a thimble and some wool wrapped around a card for darning.

Had the Ripper taken her money?

After all, she was a prostitute and had been working all night.

Surely, she would have some money on her person.

Is this another indicator that the killer was farming his victims for money?

None of the victims had a penny on them, had they all been picked clean?

If so the Ripper, who the press painted as a well to do aristocrat or doctor was certainly not well off at all.

Just as the police were getting stuck into examining the body of Liz Stride a cry came up that there had been another killing.

Abberline and his key men left the site of the murder to rush to Kearley and Tongue's warehouse in Mitre Square, where the night watchman had found a body.

Coincidentally, dozens of police were on duty in that area to try and deter the killer and one had found an apron next to an open door.

There above it, written with white chalk on a black wall, *'The Juwes are the men that will not be blamed for nothing'*

Detective Hunt ordered that it be photographed and washed off.

Such outpourings of a racist kind were sadly commonplace in Whitechapel in those days, but unlikely to have been the Ripper. His passion was of a far bloodier nature.

Yet the press and the locals would use this as another excuse to persecute the Jewish population.

Incidents included smashing windows, beating them on the streets and several stabbings of innocent men and boys.

The apron, however, had been cut off the victim and had been used to wipe the Ripper's hands after a particularly bloody nights work. So if the Ripper had taken a victims apron, did he choose to place it beneath the racist chalking? If so was it because he agreed with the sentiment, or the certain knowledge if the police were looking for a Jewish man, they were further away from catching him?

There was no trouble identifying the woman, a mustard tin found next to her body had pawn tickets made out to two women; Jane Kelly and Emily Binell.

Both names were made up, yet the items pawned were a pair of man's boots and a white flannel shirt, along with other items stolen from a punter after she had sex with them. Catherine Eddowes had often called herself Kelly or Kate Conway, Kate Convy, Katie Connaughty, Katherine Conn, Catherine McCann and many others, so she could not be traced after robbing a client.

The boots belonged to an ex-boyfriend of seven years, John Kelly, who it appears had been pimping her out and had told her not to be killed by the Ripper.

Catherine had laughed at this saying "Don't you fear for me, I'll take care of myself, I'll not fall into his hands!"

Could John Kelly be the killer?

After all his meal ticket had left him.

Not only that but she had pinched his best boots too.

An article in the East London Observer declared that Eddowes knew her killer and that the knowledge would get her killed. Was this true or had her ex, Kelly, used this as a way of making money from reporters? Could it even had been because he had been Ripper?

On the night concerned, Catherine had been arrested for being drunk and disorderly after

boozing away the profits of her long nights illicit sex.

She was still happy when after a couple of hours she was released from Bishopsgate Police Station.

'Good night old cock' she shouted to the desk sergeant then blew him a kiss.

She was back on her patch of Mitre Square by around 1am.

Three men, who had been drinking at the Imperial Club, had spotted a man and woman on the edge of the square. The man was not well dressed, aged around 30 and 5 foot eight.

He had a fair complexion and small moustache.

When the men appeared, he turned his face away and walked with Catherine into Mitre Square. This was usual behaviour for married men, not wishing for friends or family spotting them purchasing sex from the cheap Whitechapel women.

As the apron was not there at 2.20am but was at 2.55am it is fair to assume the murder was done in enough time for the killer to make his escape between these times.

Catherine Eddowes sad end was ably described with Doctor Brown's initial report.

Brown noted

> 'The body was on its back, arms by her sides. There was a thimble on one finger of her right hand. The clothes were pulled up above the abdomen, the thighs were naked, the left thigh extended in line with the body. The right leg bent at the knee. There was great disfigurement of the face. The throat cut across, the intestines had been drawn out and placed over her right shoulder, and they were smeared with faecal matter. Two feet of intestines were cut out and placed between the body and the left arm. The lobe and auricle of the right ear had been cut through and removed. There was a huge pool of blood flowing under the neck down to below the right shoulder.'

In fact the blood pool was still trickling when the body was found. This was certain proof the murder was fresh, and probably that the Ripper was nearby. Enjoying the shock and horror caused by his work to the ordinary folk who found poor Catherine.

The post-mortem was rather more graphic adding the following perversions:

> 'The knife across the throat had cut down to the

> spine. The stomach had been cut upwards from the genitals to the chest. The liver had been sliced in two from within.'

The murderer had almost cut out the vagina and rectum. Dozens of separate cuts, incisions, slicing as if he was toying with her in the same way you would a rat in a biology lesson at school.

He had the power to do anything to this woman, and some of it whilst the victim is still alive and could feel every vicious slicing touch.

Following this slaying the killer would have been covered in blood. The left kidney had been removed, the womb cut through and much of it taken.

For the first time, the Ripper had attacked the victims face in a merciless assault.

Had he known the victim, or had the victim recognised him?

It is known in forensic circles that if a killer is recognised he needs to disassociate with the victim. So using knives, rocks, crude implements to render his prey unrecognisable.

In this case, he had cut into both her eyes.

Many newspapers had said that the last image seen by a murder victim is left captured on their eyes. Only the less well educated believed this, but was this just in case?

There was a deep cut over the bridge of Catherine's nose all the way down to her jaw.

The tip of the nose was detached, another stabbed through the face and across the gum.

In total about fourteen wounds had been delivered to the face turning it into mulch.

The doctors universally agreed that this man had NO surgical expertise at all.

He was not a doctor, nor was he a butcher. The press ignored this choosing to point fingers at anyone interested in medicine or in the butchery or tanning crafts.

It is safe to presume the killer was polishing up his technique. Yet this was far away from even medical school basics. The killer may know basic biology, but his inexperience proved itself in him requiring to take numerous cuts to carry out a task a surgeon could do in a single stroke of a scalpel.

This time, following being disturbed, he had the audacity to use his near capture as a distraction to the police. Was this a double thrill to him? When he was almost captured before he became 'the Ripper' and someone saw his face, that made his heart race yet he carried on. No deep sunk rationale about 'wanting' to be caught. He wanted to kill and mutilate, and throughout his carnage years, it seems he did everything he could to avoid capture. So he could have gone home, escaping from yet another murder, but he wanted the exquisite sensation of power, whilst torturing and mutilating these poor dying women. So whilst all of London's Police force sought him, he had gone about procuring his next victim. This time he would have those 'private flesh peeling moments!

The missing pieces of poor Catherine Eddowes were thought to be merely a killers trophies.

However, her poor kidney would return in dramatic fashion.

On the streets there was chaos and near anarchy. Liz Stride and Catherine Eddowes were well liked in Whitechapel, their murders above any generated a genuine fear amongst the streetwalkers. Within days, a local militia was put together. Many of these men were or had been customers to the street walkers, so wanted to keep the police away from their door. In fact I believe that the Ripper was almost certainly a member of the militia, at very least he would attend their meetings and appear to be supportive of their cause.

This gang of mainly thugs began attacking foreigners, innocent butchers and pelting the coaches of any doctors passing through.

It merely added a vicious, additional strand of misinformation to muddy the waters and actually help the killer vanish back into the shadows.

CHAPTER TWENTY

GHOST HUNT 1

MITRE SQUARE STILL EXISTS TODAY, and is a modern multi-storied wall of offices and accommodation. At the time Catherine Eddowes was found in the South –West corner by the local beat bobby PC Edward Watkins making his fourth sweep of the night. I attached a recording device at about waist height on a wall, exactly where the body lay.

During the night, there were many passers by, the occasional drunken crowd and even one 'lady' who urinated there, all caught on tape. Yet even under extra scrutiny, nothing you would call other worldly.

GHOST HUNT 2JULY 2017

ON RETURNING to this Ripper kill zone I see the Council have added raised beds to Mitre Square, along with comfortable wooden benches. I recalled where the body had been left, and spent some time there trying to channel off the ground, the wall, even the old gutter where the blood would have run into. Whilst I was touching the ground, beneath where the dying woman lay, I could have sworn someone placed a hand on my shoulder. I jumped up opening my eyes but there was no one there, not even a distance away. I started recording at 1.00am, earlier than the attack, and I walked across to the wooden bench. This time I would stare at the area, and make sure no one, accidentally finds the gear and has off with it. At about 2.40am a police car stopped and a police officer asked what I was doing. As I spoke to him, I could see he was staring at something from the very corner I had been watching. "Who is with you?" he enquired. I told him I was on my own, and heading overseas the following day. He looked a little spooked before saying, "I thought I saw someone over there in that corner!" It was the precise place Catherine had been killed! I had not said where I was watching, yet had there been a dark shape moving around there? If so was it Catherine's poor spirit ripped before her time, or was it Jack's black soul following to see if I was on the right track?

I saw a few dark shapes between then and early morning. On one occasion even went up to the site and it was unbelievably cold. Yet the night was warm, temperate and even summery. On the recording, we captured incredible white noise, yet all night there had been nothing remotely like it. Then a period of quiet, like the machine was broken. Then out of that quiet the sound of a cutlery knife landing on a tiled kitchen floor. Did any of this mean anything at all? Spiritually there had been an increasing pathway, yet now things were becoming more and more frustrating.

GHOST SIGHTINGS:

ANOTHER BUSY PLACE, and when not loaded with the public, the spirits seem to visit regularly too. There is a couple who are seen arm in arm aged about 70, said to have died in a road accident nearby.

There was an incident in 1966 when a woman and three students in the flat next door, watched a woman get murdered exactly where Jack the Ripper had killed Catherine. Three teenagers were waiting for friends to come around for an ad-hoc party. Everyone was late, all stopping off at a pub first when they all watched out of the window. This woman was despatched with a knife and everyone was screaming. They called the police and did not expect that this would end up with all four being ridiculed, yet they were sure what they had seen.

Another famous ghost from the 1960's was that of 'the shadow man'. A number of women from about 1962 until 1969 kept reporting seeing a man 'hiding in bushes',' crouching in a doorway' or slowly following women on their own down the street. The man wore some kind of hat and had a long coat and carried something in his right hand. At first the police thought it was a stalker, a flasher or a potential rapist so put two officers on the case. In the first year, they never ever saw this character despite eight or night complaints across a standard week. Finally a female officer in plain clothes acted as bait, and saw a man following her along the mews into Mitre Square. She admitted being terrified yet summoned other police to attend. She claimed he had stepped into a doorway, yet that door was locked and no one seemed in. Three nights later the same police woman declared the figure to be a ghost. She spent the night standing in that doorway, right where the Ripper murder had happened. At about 1.50am a black 'thing' raced up to her, went physically through her, then through the heavy bolted door. She reported "I cannot explain the following but insist it happened, I am not on medication nor drunk however farfetched this story may appear. She then put it all in the log. Later that month she was interviewed by her Inspector who told her that her tale it was impossible. Three weeks she was transferred to the Cambridge force.

CHAPTER TWENTY-ONE

The upper echelons were becoming increasingly disturbed by reports that the police did not care for the working classes.

This was nothing in comparison with how the women of Whitechapel felt. For decades they had provided a service for every man that sought a bit of 'comfort' and were now dying because of it. They demanded help and protection, sometimes only daring to go out in two's, three's or four's.

Many would never cross the door unless they had a man by their side, or their friends. At night time the working girls continued to ply their trade, taking every safeguard possible. Some only went with a client provided that he was introduced to her colleagues or her pimp.

This put off most punters and times became desperate for prostitutes, unable to make their rent. Landlords universally ignored the Ripper as any type of excuse and dozens were evicted around this time. Inadvertently forcing the girls to walk the streets again, and putting them out for the Ripper!

The police hunt went on and the press continued to paint the picture of a well-heeled doctor hiding in the London fog to leap out on unsuspecting prostitutes.

Everything about this picture was wrong; if you follow the evidence the Ripper was not remotely wealthy. Coroners and doctors agreed he had only a basic knowledge of anatomy and witnesses to earlier crimes had all agreed on a shabbily dressed man of about 5'8".

Three days later the police found another body on the Embankment on the Thames.

A warehouse had been broken into and the torso of a young woman was uncovered. Her arms, legs or head were not anywhere to be seen.

Ten days later the arms were found further down the river but she was never identified. Most police officers refused to accept that this could be the work of the Ripper. The truth was the police had no clue to when he started, how many crimes had been committed, which ones were his and those belonging to others.

However, that did not stop the press from initially printing headlines like 'Latest Ripper Butchery', 'The Ripper Strikes Again' and even 'Police Helpless Over Ripper Massacre'.

Why let the truth get in the way of a good story?

This may have been the Ripper trying something new, yet there were none of his signature

mutilations. His ego would certainly have made him leave some clue as he toyed with a totally ineffectual police investigation. Many say he did this killing, because murderers did tend to kill in the same way. So he murdered another homeless woman in a completely different way. Was he toying with them even more?

Five weeks after the murder of Catherine Eddowes surprisingly the people of Whitechapel were beginning to think that the Ripper had left the area.

The only horrific event was a kidney that the Ripper had sent to George Lusk, unofficial leader of the unruly militia..

We will be looking at the Ripper letters later.

A whole month without a killing Maybe it was someone who had been robbed by a prostitute, who had made his point and now moved on.

Theft from a punter was commonplace.

The easiest trick was whilst the punter was on top of the woman, trousers around his ankles, it was easy to pick his pocket and hide the money or wallet in her undergarments.

So prostitutes believed he had gone, they would still steal from clients, unless it was a regular who treated them well.

At 10.45am on Friday the 9th of November John McCarthy, a local tenement landlord, was checking his books, only to discover that Mary Kelly was 29 shillings in arrears with her rent.

That was a small fortune at this time, so he sent a lackey called Bowyer to her flat to get some money. Kelly had told him she was going to watch that days Lord Mayors Parade and on getting no reply thought she may already have set off.

Many working girls merely pretended to be out to avoid the rent man, so Bowyer walked around the side of the building to a window where two of the dirty panes were broken and peered inside. As his eyes became accustomed to the darkness he saw a heap of flesh oozing blood on the table. On overcoming his shock he focused in on a bloodied body on the bed so he turned and ran.

When the police, accompanied by Dr. Phillips, pick-axed the door down it was obvious that the Ripper had been at work again.

The body was unrecognisable as a human being, had the eyes

and brow not been intact a basic identification would have been impossible.

As the room was searched scant regard was paid to the blazing fire in the hearth, so hot the spout of a kettle had melted off. This was thought to be the Ripper's work, burning wood and clothes to give him light to carry out his horrific hobby.

Yet the clothes were not just a women's, there were signs of a grubby man's jacket and shirt. The police disregarded this being the Ripper's because it was old and cheap. They were searching for someone a good sight richer. The mistake they had made from the beginning. At that very second real evidence was burning in poor Mary Jane Kelly's hearth.

Across that evening there had been a number of people who had heard 'Murder' shouted late in the night. This had been screamed by a woman at least three times. People had looked out into the yard, yet on seeing nothing had taken it no further.

On having investigated, nothing was to be found.

A number of witnesses said they had seen someone talking to Mary just before her murder, others claimed they had seen the same man earlier looking down the lane where she lived. This man did not come forward, despite exhaustive enquiries and the newspapers asking him to.

Dr.Bond, another police doctor made notes as he investigated the initial scene.

Here is part of his actual report:

> 'The body was naked in the middle of the bed, shoulders flat. The legs were wide apart and the entire surface of the abdomen and thighs were removed and the abdominal cavity emptied of its viscera.

> The breasts were cut off. the arms mutilated and the face hacked beyond recognition. The tissue of the neck was severed down to the bone. The viscera had been placed in various parts of the room. The uterus, kidneys and one breast had been put under the head, the other breast by her foot. The liver was between her feet, the intestines on her right-hand side with her spleen on the left. The flaps of skin from her thighs and abdomen had been put into piles on the table next to the window.
>
> The face was gashed in every direction following a furious assault. The nose, cheeks, eyebrows and ears had all been partially removed. The lips were cut several times all the way down to her chin'

There was one mistake in his report, Mary was in fact wearing a small chemise style corset that had been obscured by the blood. Once again the destruction of the face suggests that the killer knew his victim and was trying to remove any trace of her, for he would feel guilt mutilating her if she was a 'friendly' dead face.

As the inquest began, some of the witnesses were whispering that the witness who had not come forward was George Hutchinson. Realising the police would soon come knocking he walked into Commercial Street police station.

He had already been questioned by police near the scene and had told them he was nowhere near and did not know Mary Kelly.

Here is the statement he made, completely changing the story:

> 'At 2.00am I met with the murdered woman Kelly and she said "Hutchinson will you lend me sixpence?" I told her I couldn't. I had spent all my money going

down to Romford. She said "Good morning then, I must go and find some money". She walked towards Thrawl Street and a man tapped her on the shoulder. They both burst out laughing and I heard her say 'Alright'" He then put his hand around her shoulders. He also carried a small parcel in his left hand with a strap around it. I was standing under the lamp of the Queens Head Public House and watched them. They came past me and his head was stooped down, hat over his eyes and I bent down and looked at his face. It seemed stern. They went into Dorset Street and I followed some way behind. They stood on the corner for a few minutes And I heard her say 'Alright my dear come along, you shall be comfortable'. He put his arm on her shoulder and kissed her, he pulled out his red handkerchief and gave it to her. They went down into her court, I stood there for 45 minutes but they did not come out, so I went away.

The man was about 5'6" and 34 or 35 years of age with dark complexion and a dark moustache turned up at the ends. He had long eyelashes and blue eyes. He was wearing a long dark coat trimmed with astrakhan fur. He had a white collar, black necktie in which he had affixed a horseshoe pin. He wore a pair of dark spats with light buttons over button boots. Displayed from his waistcoat was a massive gold chain. His watch chain had a big seal with a red stone hanging from it. He had a heavy moustache, dark eyes and bushy eyebrows. He had no side whiskers and his chin was clean shaven. He looked like a foreigner. The small parcel he carried was about

> eight inches long. It looked as if it was covered in American cloth. He had brown gloves, he walked very softly and I believe he lives in the neighbourhood, and I fancied that I saw him in Petticoat Lane on Sunday morning.'

LATER HE TOLD his friends in a local bar "You have to tell the police everything or this brute will kill off all our friendly girls, then where will we be!"

Inspector Abberline saw this statement as a major break-through and was now more sure he would capture the gentleman killer. On the 19th of November thousands lined the route as poor Mary Kelly's body was taken for burial to St. Patrick's Roman Catholic Cemetery in Leytonstone.

Many say the Ripper was certainly in the crowd, amused at all the fuss he had caused. I believe that not only that I think he probably followed the cortege all the way to the cemetery, surprised at how poor prostitutes were having almost a state funeral.

CHAPTER TWENTY-TWO

GHOST HUNT 1

NUMBER 13 MILLER'S COURT is now a long road of four storey buildings, yet at the time it was bedraggled single bedroom flat. The guts of it remains today, despite incredible modernising around it. I found the long tunnel walkway that took you to where the house should be. Thanks to a local landlord was allowed into the modern flat that was on the site of the place where Mary was butchered. The recording gave me heavy slamming and banging, impossible not to wake everyone in the area. The noises then stopped and I heard what was like a girl or young woman whimpering. There are spirit of every kind all over, so put it down to a passing spirit. Yet could it have been Mary?

GHOST HUNT 2JULY 2017

ON RETURNING, I located the owners of the property who told me that they were in for the night, sleeping in upstairs rooms. They allowed me to have all of the downstairs to place my devices. I caught their bedtime toilet breaks, and in the middle of a confusing number of noises all on top of one another a woman say "It's YOU!... it's you!" Then a whole collection of noises cover up the crackly voice that continued. Then the machine jammed and drained of all of its energy. It this was from Mary Jane Kelly she clearly knew her killer!

SIGHTINGS:

I ENQUIRED if spiritualists had ever carried out an exorcism of the area and it has never been. Instead the clergy tend to get sucked in by the bloody enamour of the Ripper, and find themselves seeking more information. It seems in the early 1900's Sir Arthur Conan Doyle (not confirmed but likely knowing his obsession with the case) may well have sent local spiritualists from their local branch. They claimed it was an ugly, scar faced man who will not leave. One woman claimed this is where 'bad things' had been done but had no idea. It was a dozen years since the Ripper; his name was no longer the draw it used to be.

Yet in 1934, William Rush took his father to London to check out an apartment for his family, should he get the promotion he sought. He was going up in the world and moving to the London branch of his chain of Insurance brokers. He looked at the flat two streets from Miller's Court, then on liking the property he remembered seeing a fish and chippy nearby, so took a short cut along Miller's Court. His little boy raced behind him, both hungry and looking forward to their supper. Two thirds of the way down that street, the boy cried out and fell to the ground. Rush turned and picked up his little boy and when he looked at his injuries under a streetlight, his left eyeball had been cut in two. He looked around to see what had caused this, yet there was nothing at all capable of such an injury.

The following morning police searched the area, they too were unable to find anything that could have blinded that little boy in one eye. The case was left 'open'.

Yet when people enquire about just how dangerous ghosts are, they should consider cases like this, instead of always bleating, "It's the living you want to worry about not the dead!"

So now, back to our hunt for the Ripper.

CHAPTER TWENTY-THREE

The following day, perhaps spurred on by his increasing celebrity, he had he struck again. Working girl Annie Farmer picked up a client who she had often seen in Whitechapel.

Two hours later she ran out of her kitchen bleeding from a wound in her throat.

Other lodgers in the George Street house raced to help her but the man ran from the house fully clothed into Thrawl Street and vanished in the crowds.

Annie said the man was about middle thirties, 5'6" to 5'8", dark complexion, black moustache and no side whiskers. He was wearing a shabby suit, a battered black felt hat and looked common but respectable.

The police thought this to be a pimp trying to get more money from his whores, as some girls hid coins from them by concealing them in their mouths.

Yet was it the Ripper seeking another kill?

CHAPTER TWENTY-FOUR

The most infamous Ripper letter was sent to the leader of the Whitechapel Vigilance Committee, George Lusk, along with part of a human kidney taken from the body of Catherine Eddowes. This would be known for all time as the 'From Hell' letter:

'FROM HELL

Mr Lusk Sor,

I send you half the kidne I took from one woman prasarved it for you tother piece I fried and ate it was very nise. I may send you the bloody knif that I took it out with if you will only wate a whil longer.

Signed

catch me when you can Mishter Lusk.'

MANY BELIEVE the writer could spell but chose to misspell.

However, following the kidney's inclusion there was no doubt this man was the Ripper.

Dr. Openshaw confirmed the kidney was Catherine Eddowes' left kidney that had been cut out probably while she was still alive. This led to him receiving a letter from Jack:

'Old Boss you was rite it was the left kidney I was going to hopperate agin close to your ospitle just as I was going to draw my nife along of er bloomin throte them cusses of coppers spoilt the game but I guess I will be on the job soon and I will send you another bit of innerds.

Jack the Ripper

PS

O have you seen the devle
With his mikerscope and scalpel
a-lookin at a kidney
With a slide cocked up.'

THIS LETTER IS proof that the writer was more literate than he tried to suggest. In previous letters he knew knife began with a 'k' and he correctly spells kidney, when previously he did not.

After the death of Mary Kelly and an attack on Annie Farmer a letter written on a newspaper arrived. Marked 'Liverpool':

'DEAR BOSS

Look out on the 7th inst. Am trying my hand at disjointing and if I can manage it will

send you a finger.

Yours truly, Jack the Ripper.'

SO NOW YOU have had the Rippers own clues. However, we must also remember that in more recent times the Yorkshire Ripper investigation was sent on a wild goose chase following receipt of a tape recording thought to come from Sunderland, where a man claimed to be the Yorkshire Ripper. Eventually the hoax was revealed but literally hundreds of man hours were wasted whilst Peter Sutcliffe continued to kill.

CHAPTER TWENTY-FIVE

A month to the day, in November, the police found another body.

She had not been robbed as she had one shilling and tuppence in her purse.

Her clothes seemed undisturbed.

The woman was Rose Mylett, a woman thought to be a prostitute.

Earlier that evening she had been approached by two sailors and heard to shriek at them 'No! No! No!'. Hours later those sailors had found a willing woman and had caroused in the George Public House on Commercial Road so are unlikely murderers.

Initially it was thought that a ligature had strangled Rose and thumb marks were found on her neck.

Later the marks were said to be commonplace on women wearing stiff starched collars.

Other doctors said she had choked on her own vomit whilst

drunk, yet a verdict of murder by some person or persons unknown was eventually given by the Coroner.

Was this totally unrelated, or had the Ripper tried to throttle another woman before toying with her? Did this killer, who had prided himself in not getting blood on himself decide to stop this attack for she had vomited on him?

Six long months passed and more body parts were found in the Thames belonging to Elizabeth Jackson. The parts were wrapped in her clothes and showed signs of mutilation and amputation. The crime was never seriously linked to the Ripper. Should it have been?

On checking at that time around forty bodies were found, many cut to pieces or mutilated during the time of the Ripper. How many serial killers were there in that tiny area of the Capital?

As always the police had more questions than answers.

Six months without a proven ripping, had the Ripper left London?

The newspapers gave lists of foreigners who had travelled to America or who had returned to Europe asking if they could be Jack the Ripper?

The police had downgraded the investigation.

After all the killings had stopped and the murderer had not actually killed anyone important, it was the obvious thing to do.

This would lead many to believe that the Ripper had been someone famous, a freemason, an aristocrat, a Royal maybe. Why else would they stop looking for such a bloody and disgusting killer?

Death leaves a stain. Disturbed spirits seeking justice. Yet the stench of death would return to Whitechapel, the Ripper was not finished yet!

CHAPTER TWENTY-SIX

It had been some seven months since Mary Kelly had been hacked to pieces.

Other bodies had been found yet, still the police manipulated the spin to try a calm the fears of the people of Whitechapel.

Sergeant Edward Badham had experienced the Ripper's brutality face on. He had already had the dubious pleasure of taking the blood-soaked corpse of Annie Chapman to the morgue. He said it was an image that haunted his every dream!

He had just exchanged words with one of his constables, Walter Andrews, as they walked past one another on Castle Alley. Seconds later Andrews saw the bleeding body of a woman. How had the Sergeant missed it?

Right from the beginning a police officer or police doctor had been on the list of suspects. Badham had been at or near at least four of the murders. Yet whilst looking at the bleeding body, obviously not long dead, he heard footsteps further along the alley.

Instead of following police procedure and stay with the body,

Andrews was up on his toes and giving chase. They found a couple of local men claiming to be going to McCarthy's the Chandler, the man who was Mary Kelly's landlord. Their names were never taken, but they were identified as people who had previously given statements to the police. The policeman was out of breath and as there were two men, and of course Jack always worked alone, he never thought for a second that he may have just let the Ripper walk away!

Suddenly it began to rain heavily and the evidence along with the victim's blood began to run along the gutters of Whitechapel. Like all the Ripper victims the head had been turned to the right and there was a deep incisive wound to her throat.

The ladies clothing had been pulled back and underwear removed. There was a wound in the abdomen but no sign of mutilation. It was as if the killer had been disturbed, and not for the first time.

The woman was eventually identified as Alice McKenzie. Alice had occasionally worked as a prostitute but had been Jiving with a fellow and trying to manage without doing that.

The police pathologist, who had been ordered to downplay the Ripper murders, declared that this was another killer. However, Dr. Bond who had examined previous victims told the press that he had no doubt that it was Jack the Ripper's handiwork. The coroner told the police he was certain it was the Ripper's handiwork. They chose to downplay it, wanting to believe it was just a random attack. Jack the Ripper had gone. They were determined to leave it that way.

Subsequently officers agreed that the political pressure put on detectives had made it impossible for them to catch the real killer.

There were even more twists and turns to come, for on Sunday the 8th September 1889 a man in New York called John Cleary waltzed into the office of the New York Herald and declared that Jack the Ripper had struck again.

He said that London police had found another body in White Horse Yard, near where Liz Stride had been butchered.

At first this was treated as a hoax until, in Pinchin Street, they found the torso of a woman. Her head and legs had been removed. There was no blood anywhere and the body had begun to rot. The strench was vile, creeping around the chest and making at least one officer vomit. The cause of death had been a violent cut across the throat, identical to Ripper attacks on at least three earlier victims.

There was no mutilation but in at least two previous cases the killer had tried to remove the heads of Mary Kelly and before that Annie Chapman.

There was a rip right down the centre of the abdomen exposing the intestines but this time none had been removed.

John Cleary knew of the body, yet it had not officially been found.

How did he know?

He was either the killer, the Ripper, or knew who was.

Finally, a news vendor claimed he had made up the name Cleary and whilst living in London had heard a man in uniform say "Hurry there has been another horrible murder". Once again a news man just before leaving London, used a little information to make a few pounds. These were the things that deflected police from seeking out the real killer.

CHAPTER TWENTY-SEVEN

So, the puzzle becomes even more complex.

Was the killer a policeman?

Did the police find the body earlier but choose to hide it, so the Ripper legend would not get even further out of hand?

Arnold described the man as early thirties wearing a dark uniform.

His height was around 5' 8" with a fair complexion and a moustache. He was carrying a small paper parcel around eight inches in length. His clothes were rather tatty and old.

Was the Ripper posing as a police officer to attract his victims?

Dozens of other prostitutes were missing but an official identification of this body was never made.

By now the press were also off track by accepting weak police evidence, distancing the Pinchin Street torso from the Ripper investigation.

They ran a story asking readers if they knew a husband who no longer lived with his wife. They believed the murder to be a domestic incident. This completely ignores the facts. Realistically the police believed the Ripper had stopped long ago and had left the area, died or returned to his previous life. They were soon to be regretting their stance on the evening before Valentine's Day in 1891 - over two years later.

Ernie Thompson had only been a policeman for about a year when he was given his first ever nightshift. At 2.15am he was walking his beat and on entering Swallow Gardens he heard footsteps racing away from him.

As he tried to focus beneath the dim streetlights he saw a woman in great distress.

The woman's throat had been sliced and blood was pouring from the wound. Being new he was unsure whether to run after the fleeing person, or try to give medical assistance to the woman soaked in her own blood.

This rookie was in shock too, blowing his whistle over and over again as the woman opened her eyes and locked him in a deathly stare.

Dr. Oxley was first in attendance and declared the throat had been cut in a sawing motion as if it had been an attempt to remove it.

By now that dim spark of life had been extinguished in poor Frances Cole.

It was obvious that the murderer had been disturbed and her clothes had not been removed, nor had the lower body been mutilated. It seems that it was becoming harder for the killer to find anywhere he could be left long enough to mutilate his victims anymore.

On these facts alone it was discounted as a Ripper killing. The police were desperate to continue believing that he had gone long ago.

Yet, as was Jack's custom, if he does not torture, he will have another try that evening. That is precisely what happened. A woman, some caller her Susan Aitkin, a nanny was on her way home after visiting a sick relative. She came face to face with a tatty, wild eyed man with a poc marked face, broad moustache and newspaper parcel. He pushed her into a doorway, to his surprise the door opened, as the house owner was heading out to work. In that moment of screaming, shoving and the owner falling backwards into his own hall, the man disappeared into the foggy evening. Susan Aitkin reported it to a beat bobby who logged it, but did not report it to the Ripper team.

Out of all the crimes that were committed in Whitechapel you now have all those that are or could have been associated with Jack the Ripper.

So, who were the real suspects?

Let us round on them in true Agatha Christie style.

CHAPTER TWENTY-EIGHT

The search of a monster, a man who slaughtered women and hideously mutilated their bodies. Surely that should be the easiest thing to do once you have your suspects gathered like Hercule Poirot in the drawing room of fiction?

Yet the truth is that almost any one of the suspects could have done it, it is now up to you to decide who Jack the Ripper was.

The only thing I have not provided you with is the alibis for all of the contenders.

Once you have that information then you can name who the Ripper is, and you will have been armed with more information than the police at the time of the killings.

CHAPTER TWENTY-NINE

The first name has to be the Duke of Clarence.

As a Royal living in London at a time of extreme poverty the jealousy of the poor pushed him to the very top of the list. However, he knew nothing of Whitechapel's back streets, the alleys and back lanes that had allowed the killer to escape on at least four occasions.

He was said to be a gentle and reserved man. Funny with a kindness towards people.

He may have been bisexual as he often 'entertained' men and women.

So, what proof was there?

After an early murder a witness saw the Royal coach drive by.

They had no idea who was in it, but the Duke admitted it was he.

He had occasionally joined a number of aristocrats for a night of 'whoring' after slipping out of the Palace.

In effect, not one shred of evidence, but it allowed the press to have a field day at his expense.

He had no motive.

Take this a step further and look at crimes that he could not have committed.

He was out of London on at least four of the attacks, and has witnesses in Scotland to prove it. However, with his status he could buy an alibi.

SIR WILLIAM GULL is the next possible killer.

Many said that he was going out with the Duke, to cover up the heinous hobby of the Royal. Then the Freemasons were charged with protecting the killer who was one of their numbers. They would never betray a fellow of the Lodge not for 'a few filthy prostitutes'. Once again the press are thought to have invented the initial hoax tying Gull to the Prince and tying in the Freemasons.

The impoverished were happy to believe the killer to be one of the rich, rather than someone living amongst them.

Gull was a good doctor, brilliantly skilled, humane without any trace of motive.

His fitness was very poor, if he walked thirty yards he was panting due to a lung condition.

It was impossible for him to run or climb fences.

Once again there is no proof whatsoever against him.

Whilst two of the victims were being ripped he was delivering babies.

Or was this a fiction to cover the fact that he had blood on him?

DOCTOR ROSLYN D'ONSTUN lived in Whitechapel, he knew it well and had nerves of steel.

But, in fact, his real name was Robert Donston Stephenson. He got into the occult and began to re-style his image in keeping with the likes of Aleister Crowley the other Satanist. He was a calculating ex-soldier known for meticulous planning in his military campaigns and even though he seemed fit he was 47 years old.

Could he really outrun a 23-year old policeman'?

He was also 5'10" and wore heeled boots making him look at least six foot tall.

The motive given to him was that he sought power for his perverted black magic delusions. However, he was never remotely involved in black magic ceremonies involving blood sacrifices of any living things.

A rumour abounded from an ex-girlfriend that he had a box full of bloody ties, perhaps dipped in the blood of each victim as a trophy.

This was never proven and it was later discovered the girlfriend sold the story to the press. Later Aleister Crowley claimed he had once owned the box of ties, but at that time he was trying to build up his image as Britain's leading occultist and had also claimed to have owned Excalibur. He had dumped his girlfriend and this could easily have been the vengeful action of a woman scorned.

He wrote about the murders in the press. Was this the perfect cover for the killer?

JAMES STEPHEN WAS ALSO CONSIDERED to be the Ripper. On one occasion, a crowd pelted him with vegetables and stones when he walked through Whitechapel market.

He was a homosexual who hated women, following a childhood raised by an abusive woman. Some said that he was sold to men allowed to sexually abuse him; others claimed his mother was a prostitute.

He was very fit and a proven sportsman but had no knowledge of the area.

His motive could have been sheer hate against the trade his mother adopted.

However, there was no proof and he had alibis for all but one of the crimes.

He had brain damage, was driven mad and knew Druitt, another suspect.

Inspector Abberline thought it was he and Druitt working in tandem.

If one had an alibi the other would not, so could they be two killers?

WHAT OF MONTEGUE DRUITT?

He had a cursory knowledge of the area having an office on the edge of Whitechapel.

In his case his mother was driven mad and following her death he wanted to commit suicide. He loved women and certainly had no motive to kill, in fact there was no link between him and working girls.

He was found dead in the Thames on December 1888 and this was said by many to be the Ripper ending his own life. However, that does not answer the question of those attacked after that date, or was that merely copycats?

Although his name is oft mentioned the only evidence against him were a set of faked documents, created by a journalist.

SO MANY SUSPECTS, including Walter Sickert, who was linked to the Masonic Conspiracy as he was in the same Lodge as Gull.

He took lodgings after the third murder near Whitechapel, living next door to a veterinary student whose name was Hewitt (many claimed it was Druitt, just so it fits).

He was a fit man and often walked late at night in his top hat and long black coat.

There is no motive and no proof against him.

SO, we have looked at the richer suspects, what about the 'common man'?

George Hutchinson was clearly spotted near four of the killing sites just before the bodies were found. He lived in the middle of Whitechapel and everyone knew him.

He was out drinking most nights, like so many others. He was at very least a witness yet he only came forward to give a statement to the police after eight others mentioned that he was there. He was the right age, right height and knew at least three of the victims.

Mind you, most of the male residents of Whitechapel knew the working girls as they patrolled their 'patch'.

Hutchinson did not work yet always had beer money. Many believed him to be a thief and local pawnbrokers had bought rings, hatpins and jewellery from him.

FREDERICK DOWNING WAS another vicious young man. Fingers

were pointed towards him, as he hated women after being abused by his own wife.

He eventually killed her and his second wife, who was also a nag.

Then he butchered his own children so he could have a new start.

He was fit, of perfect height and build with a sworn hatred of prostitutes, as the only one he had slept with had robbed him. Many locals swore he was the Ripper but his alibi was airtight. He was in prison at the time of the killings.

ONE OF THE most likely suspects was George Chapman (real name Antoniovitch Klosowski, a Polish immigrant) who worked in Whitechapel and knew it well.

He was a calculating, manipulative and cunning man.

He lived on his wits and won a lot of money gambling and probably cheating.

He was very fit and gained pleasure from killing animals, like many killers, and gained sadistic pleasure from beating up women.

His second wife knew Annie Chapman and introduced her to George.

Over the years George had married four women, each one dying in a tragic way, yet following a post mortem poison was found.

Previous wives were dug up and his serial killing was exposed.

Poisoning was his method of killing. A cold-blooded and premeditated crime.

Not the blood-soaked frenzy of the Ripper.

He was too tall to fit the pattern and had a huge black moustache and sideburns of a vivid type. He would easily have been identified.

WILLIAM HENRY BURY was 29 at the time of the murders and once was a horsemeat butcher who used to run a brothel.

He murdered his wife by choking her with a rope, then stabbed her and wedged her into a trunk. He walked into a police station and confessed in February 1889.

On getting to his home in search of the body they found graffiti outside his door saying 'Jack the Ripper is at the back of this door' and on the stairs down to his flat more graffiti 'Jack the Ripper is in this seller!' the finger pointer was not a good speller.

His wife Ellen's body had been terribly mutilated her intestines protruding through the stomach. He was tried for her murder and hanged in Dundee on the 24th April 1889.

He was a known thief. The murders started after he arrived from Scotland and ended after he was hanged. Neighbours say it was his own wife who believed he was the Ripper, writing the graffiti herself. However, the Ripper may well have committed more attacks after that date, so it could then have been coincidental that he would butcher his wife that way. The way Jack had killed and mutilated was probably too well documented. Perhaps he was copying that style so knowing he would get the death penalty, would also become Jack The Ripper too?

Also, Bury took his wife on holiday to Wolverhampton in 1888 and whilst they were away Martha Tabram and Mary Ann Nichols were ripped.

NO WONDER the police had so much trouble.

So many potential killers, including Frederick Charrington, who was a Christian zealot, lecturing against drinking and harlots.

He was the right age, size and shape and lived alone as a celibate obsessed with the sleazy world of the Victorian prostitute. There is no proof whatsoever but his obsession made him a suspect.

AARON COHEN WAS ARRESTED in December 1888 during the police sweep of brothels following one of the murders. Many believe his other name was Aaron Kosminski.

He was in an absolute frenzy so was sent to a mental hospital, where his violent behaviour included attacking and trying to kill other patients. He died in the mental hospital the following year. Could it have been that the Ripper celebrated his murders by immediately having sex with another prostitute?

SO, who do you think it was?

You must ask yourself who is the perfect package.

Who has the motive? Who had the opportunity? Who lied?

Who could be lost in the Whitechapel crowd?

Who was Jack the Ripper?

JACK THE RIPPER UNMASKED!

CHAPTER THIRTY-ONE

I believe that right from the beginning of the police investigation they were looking for the wrong type of man. The police of that time were used to dealing with domestic incidents. Husbands killing wives, wives killing husbands, not cunning serial killers.

The streets were flooded with the police and the already crowded streets would make it impossible for any stranger not to be noticed after so many forays into a very closed community.

If we look at the search for the Yorkshire Ripper, the huge breakthrough was that cassette tape with the 'Geordie' voice. It was not even a 'Geordie' voice it was a Wearside 'Mackem' accent. Yet that one tape led to hundreds of thousands of man hours being wasted.

Anyone without a North Eastern accent was discounted, allowing Peter Sutcliffe his freedom to kill again. Sutcliffe often made deliveries to the North and had even tried to snatch two girls on the Team Valley Trading Estate in Gateshead, before he was eventually caught.

He had been interviewed by police EIGHT times.

The same level of misinformation happened back in Whitechapel.

We will capture Jack using logic and common sense. Look at the clues because they are there.

So let us put a Ripper profile together. For we now know far more than the police ever found out, with tips from experts living and beyond the grave!

> 'As a child he would kill or mutilate animals, bullying fellow schoolchildren and wishing he could kill them too. Many children would complain about beatings and bullying from this man as a boy. Most serial killers are white and begin to live out their fantasies after the age of 25. I think Jack was aged between 27 and 35. He lived in Whitechapel and his face would be known by everyone, who not only knew him but probably liked him too. Sociopaths seem to get on with everyone, yet deep below the surface there is that flip side, the Mr Hyde to his Dr.Jekyll. Many good men can kill, but in revenge or to defend their families. It takes an extremely evil creature to wish to kill in this way. Especially when you understand how importance the torturing and mutilation became. He thrived on seeing the life end as he hurt them using extraordinary techniques.
>
> He would kill where he felt safe and knew he could easily make his escape. His home was likely nearby. He would have a lowly paid job if he had a job

at all. He was certainly not in any well-paid profession. He was either very calculating or possibly a paranoid schizophrenic. There are signs of this throughout his killing spree yet he also managed to maintain incredible control. He could be ripping a woman's insides out one moment, chatting to the police next. He was quite a character. The killings were totally disorganised so the rest of his life could be too.

A tatty home, shabby clothes, no organisation in his life. His teeth would be decayed, his breath awful, hair not neatly trimmed and his personal hygiene lacking and infested with lice. His face would show signs of age or disease, poc marks were commonplace in Whitechapel at that time. Making a man in his twenties or thirties look a good twenty years older!

The prostitutes would have known him. as no decent woman would share his bed.

They would feel secure with him, as he was a local character. He was their perfect regular customer in fact. He would also visit all the pubs in Whitechapel and kept his violent tendencies well hidden. Yet he was clever, cunning and utterly without any conscience. These girls many may well have slept with him, at very least would have shared a drink or a kind word. Yet he would butcher them worse than cattle in a slaughter house.'

This discounts three quarters of the suspects at a stroke.

Any of the rich and wealthy were instantly picked out by pimps, prostitutes and the local vigilantes. Towards the latter days of the Ripper everyone was so keen on watching out, no stranger could enter Whitechapel without being challenged.

The Ripper WAS a local.

So out of the three or four local men, who lied?

Surprisingly only one, George Hutchinson, who had failed to come forward after a dozen folk saw him near Mary's murder site. When the police sought him he then came forward and gave an incredible statement, giving the perfect description of the wealthy, well to do Ripper taking Mary Kelly off to her doom.

Despite only having a split second to see the man, under dim gas lamps, he gave a four-page description of a man covering the type of jewellery he had on, his eyelashes, his cuffs, his shoes and the fact he was 'a toff'.

This statement alone led to thousands of wasted man hours. Echoes of that Yorkshire Ripper case again.

Why would you make all that up unless you had something to hide?

Was this to cover the fact that you were there next to the scene where a murder would be committed?

The first attack was not a fatal one, but Annie Millwood was attacked within two blocks of where Hutchinson lived. When she eventually died, Hutchinson would have gained confidence from this. I bet he was amazed he could murder on his own doorstep yet still be invisible to everyone including the police.

Hutchinson's next victim was Martha Tabram, just around the corner from his home.

Then going a little further away to despatch Mary Ann Nichols in Bucks Row.

This would lead on to his greatest mutilation so far, Annie Chapman, and the stealing of her rings. Almost all the victims had been without a penny on them, at a time of night when they would have been carrying all the profits of a nights work.

This killer was also a thief, maybe even living on his murderous booty. The police never ever considered that the killer may well be starting this to milk prostitutes purses, living in an area where he saw them making a lot of money every evening. There were always tales of girls 'impressing or satisfying' their clients so much they were given jewels off the rich and wealthy. Along with the money in their purses maybe enough to keep a man in a reasonable lifestyle without necessitating that he works. The women were always discovered with nothing of value, even the ones where he was disrupted. Thus proving how important cash was to the killer. A point no one seem to have realised!

Then on to the mutilation of Catherine Eddowes, but he was clumsy getting faecal matter on his hands from ripping open her bowel.

He wiped his hands on cloth cut from her clothes. The cloth was dropped on a direct line between the murder and Hutchinson's home. A direct arrow to his house yet it never seemed to interest the police. They never tumbled.

All these killings, whilst the police and public searched for 'the toff' carrying the little doctors bag.

Liz Stride, Annie Farmer, Rose Mylett and Elizabeth Jackson all suffered at his hands. Hutchinson's confidence must have made him think he was immortal.

Working as a Talk Show Host for more than forty years, I have met people who do things that can so easily give them a God complex. In this case a common man, feeding off his kills, yet enjoying the tinkering with the dead bodies. All within clear sight. The people saw him with the girls regularly, the police saw him and interviewed him a few times. He hid right out in the open and everyone yet no one saw him!

Even though the Police could prove he was actually in the courtyard near Mary Kelly they still had not arrested him. He was sufficiently cocky to kill Alice McKenzie almost within sight of his front door.

According to the census of 1891 George Hutchinson was no longer in London.

His neighbours said he left in 1889 around October.

Around the provinces others were ripped, in America too.

This man George Hutchinson is the only one who fits.

He lived almost in the centre of the area where the rippings were done and was so well known he could be invisible. He was the right age, height, weight and certainly fit enough. He was not a madman, nor would he be a man to take his own life. He enjoyed the game far too much. The only reason he would stop is for purely self-preservation.

CHAPTER THIRTY-TWO

GHOST HUNT FINALE.

FOLLOWING the use of a Northern medium, sadly long departed Connie Leigh of Seaton Delaval, she wrote the following:-

> "Having listened to the early tapes without knowing any of the suspects, I can tell you that we are looking for a surly man. A man with a scarred face from a heavy working background. He has no wife and lives right in the middle of where the murders took place, and we will never discover just how many he killed. Certainly over 30 all girls and older women. He used

> to cut them into pieces, but enjoyed working close up where he could see genuine terror, and kept them alive longer. I think he was in his early forties and I can see a knife in a wall, dry plaster hiding it. Still there in a Square. I see a stone with initials G and H on it. I see more bodies in a river never found, yet some mutilated, eaten away, lost in silt."

SHE THEN BEGAN TO CRY, "How can anyone do this to innocent women? This man lost his Mother as a child; he was raised by men and grew up hating women who stole from men. His Father died of drink after a woman took everything from him. The woman left him nothing except an angry little boy full of hate towards women! When his Father died he was a time bomb waiting to explode, yet cunning too! He's dead now this man, it was a long time ago. Such rage……..I have never felt such rage in an ordinary man!"

She had not read the book, yet purely through touching the recording equipment, she 'felt' things. She puts her finger right on it, such rage in an 'ordinary' man! Yet was she right about Hutchinson's upbringing?

Hutchinson's Mother walked out on the family due to her husband's brutality. His subsequent affair with a street woman caused him to lose his 'nest egg', stolen along with all his valuables whilst he was out at work. He became an alcoholic, and he was already a brute and young George regularly endured vicious beatings. Yet he never blamed his Dad he blamed 'that woman' for making him like that! At no time did she mention his name yet if she is right, there is a blade hidden in a crime scene that was used by Jack the Ripper!

Could Buckingham Palace have a cobble with the initials G &

H written on it? We only gained the information about the cobble years after Connie Leigh had died. Yet all those years before she had predicted it.

CHAPTER THIRTY-THREE

So as for Hutchinson we have a few big questions remaining.

WHERE DID HE GO?

DID HE HAVE CHILDREN?

ARE THEY OUT THERE CARRYING THAT MURDEROUS SPARK?

ONE DARK NIGHT on a narrow street as the fog rolls in perhaps one unlucky woman may find out to her cost. We will listen out for her scream.

ABOUT THE AUTHOR

Alan Robson MBS is Britain's longest running Talk Show host. He has won more awards than any other broadcaster and is especially known for his excellent interview technique and for hosting special shows involving the paranormal and esoteric. He qualified as an Exorcist in 2000 and is greatly loved by his audience of millions.

Despite offers from ALL the leading national players, Alan has remained as Metro Radio/TFM's flagship show for over 40 years, making it Britain's most listened to.

His first television show was 'PERSONAL CALL' with Nina Myskow. He then 17 series in a row on Tyne Tees/Yorkshire, including 'Robson's People' 7 series (12 episodes each), 'Robson's College Cuisine' (I series 18 episodes) and Trouble in Store BBC 1 (1 series 12 episodes).

American heavyweights, Fox became aware of his talents and hired him as host of 'SCARIEST PLACES ON EARTH' with Linda Blair. It became the most viewed 'phenomenon' show in the US and created so much interest Alan was invited onto 'LARRY KING LIVE' on CNN

In total, Alan hosted 3 massive series on Fox, then SYFY, Bravo and ABC.

Upon returning to the UK, Alan participated in 'BRITAIN AT

NIGHT' for ITV, vowing not to return to TV in Britain until he could find a production outfit capable of matching those he worked with in the USA. Despite numerous offers, he has stayed true to his word.

His press career is equally impressive, with his Alan's first commissions for English speaking newspapers across the world. Soon he was a regular in 'The Hong Kong Star' 'The Bangkok Press' and dozens of others worldwide.

The Sunday Sun hired him as 'Personal Columnist' for 11 years, following which he became a main feature writer for 13 years

The News Of The World regularly ran his ghost stories, including a month long series in their colour magazine of his 'GRISLY TALES'.

His book career has spanned decades following his original signing by Richard Branson. During this time, he wrote:-

GRISLY TRAILS & GHOSTLY TALES (No 1 Best Seller)
128,000 copies sold.
NIGHTMARE ON YOUR STREET (No1 Best Seller)
136,000 copies sold
SIMPLY THE BEST (Christmas Joke Book)
76,000 copies sold
THE LIVES AND LOVES OF A NIGHT OWL
(Hardback Autobiography) 56,000 copies sold.

For almost thirty years Alan hosted live gigs across the world, performing with Bob Dylan, Santana, Queen (5 times) ROD STEWART (3 times) BRYAN ADAMS (4 Times) TINA TURNER

(5 times) SIMPLY RED, DAVID BOWIE, GUN'S N ROSES and hundreds more.

He took part in numerous local productions culminating in his role as 'Frank.N.Furter in 'THE ROCKY HORROR SHOW, has appeared in countless pantomimes and was recently awarded the RADIO ACADEMY LIFETIME ACHIEVEMENT AWARD and given entry into NATIONAL RADIO HALL OF FAME

He was given an MBE from Her Majesty The Queen for services to broadcasting.

WALKING IN THE FOOTSTEPS OF:- JACK THE RIPPER is the first in a series which will include RASPUTIN, GILLES DE RAIS, THE REAL KING ARTHUR, ROBIN HOOD, ADOLF HITLER and ANNE FRANK.

An audio book of Alan visiting the places where Jack The Ripper struck, plus the noises they captured during a ghost hunt can be found on www.robsonsworld.co.uk

www.robsonsworld.co.uk

24883948R00068

Printed in Great Britain
by Amazon